DAVID HERBERT DONALD

LINCOLN

RECONSIDERED

David Herbert Donald is the author of many books on the Civil War era, including the Pulitzer Prize–winning *Charles Sumner and the Coming of the Civil War*, and *Lincoln*, which received the Lincoln Prize of the Lincoln and Soldiers Institute of Gettysburg College. He won a second Pulitzer Prize for *Look Homeward: A Life of Thomas Wolfe*.

LINCOLN

RECONSIDERED

DAVID HERBERT DONALD

LINCOLN
RECONSIDERED

ESSAYS ON THE CIVIL WAR ERA

VINTAGE BOOKS

A DIVISION OF RANDOM HOUSE, INC.

NEW YORK

VINTAGE BOOKS EDITION, FEBRUARY 2001

Library of Congress Cataloging-in-Publication Data
Donald, David Herbert, 1920–
Lincoln reconsidered: essays on the Civil War era / David Donald
–[3rd ed., en 1]
p. cm.
This ed. first published in 1961.
Bibliography: p.
Includes index. ISBN 0-375-72532-6: $13.00
1. Lincoln, Abraham, 1809–1865   2. United States—Politics and
government—Civil War, 1861–1865.   I. Title.
E457.8D69   1989
973.7—dc 19
CIP

Book design by Cathryn S. Aison

Printed in the United States of America
10 9 8 7 6 5 4 3 2

FOR AÏDA

CONTENTS

Contents

PREFACE

ALFRED A. KNOPF, surely the greatest American publisher, had a pawky sense of humor. He had published my first book, *Lincoln's Herndon*, in 1948, and in 1955 I presented for his consideration a collection of my essays on Abraham Lincoln and the Civil War. He liked the essays but was troubled that I didn't have a title for the book. After ruminating for several minutes, he announced, in all apparent seriousness, that he would call it "Chips from a Historian's Workbench."

Fortunately his marketing department shot down that idea, and when the essays were published the next year they bore the title *Lincoln Reconsidered*. The book was so successful that in 1961 a second edition was called for, in which I included two additional essays. And now here is a third edition, which includes two hitherto unpublished essays: "Education Defective: Lincoln's Preparation for Greatness," and "Reverence for the Laws: Abraham Lincoln and the Founding Fathers."*

Glad as I am that the book was not sunk by Alfred Knopf's suggested title, I can see—in retrospect, at least—that it had considerable merit. If not exactly chips from my workbench, the essays in

---

*I have omitted from this edition "Toward a Western Literature" (written in collaboration with Frederick A. Palmer).

Lincoln Reconsidered represent investigations that had to be made, problems that had to be solved, before I could proceed with the large biographies of Charles Sumner and Abraham Lincoln, on which I was engaged. For instance, "Toward a Reconsideration of Abolitionists" emerged from my attempt to understand why Charles Sumner, like so many other New Englanders of his generation, became such a passionate advocate of the abolition of slavery. Similarly, "Refighting the Civil War" resulted from my effort to understand the strategy and tactics of Union generals so that I could better appraise Lincoln's role in directing the war. Several of the other essays—especially "The Radicals and Lincoln"—were intended to clear the ground for my Lincoln biography by analyzing Civil War political leadership.

Originating in my own need for self-education, these essays had an added objective: I wanted to share my excitement over applying methods derived from the other social sciences to knotty, much controverted historical problems. Thus, in "Getting Right with Lincoln" and "The Folklore Lincoln" I tried to show how the methods of cultural anthropologists and folklorists can reveal new ways of thinking about the Lincoln symbol. I applied the techniques of psychology and sociology to explore the origins of the abolitionist movement and borrowed from political science the technique of career-line analysis to identify the Radical Republicans. In "Refighting the Civil War" I wanted to show that military history, so often treated as a narrow, isolated specialty, has significant connections with intellectual history and the history of technology. My several studies of Lincoln as wartime political leader suggest how political theory can help recast our assumptions about the nature of nineteenth-century American political parties.

Though a slim book, *Lincoln Reconsidered* has had considerable impact on the study of the Civil War era. Widely used in colleges, and even in high schools, it has stimulated other historians to think afresh about the period. For instance, my stress on the importance of the Lincoln legend—on what people believe Lincoln said and did, whether accurate or not—helped call attention to the importance of studying the Lincoln myth. Merrill D. Peterson's richly rewarding *Lincoln in American Memory* (1994) has carried this exploration much further, and David W. Blight's *Race and Reunion: the Civil War in American Memory* offers a searching analysis. My essay on abolitionists evoked a good deal of criticism, but it also led other historians to treat the antislavery crusade as social movement, rather than as a morality play. Similarly, even when scholars disagreed with the conclusions in "Refighting the Civil War," they went on to investigate the intellectual background of Civil War military leaders and to discuss their theories of warfare. "A Whig in the White House" may not have originated the recent re-evaluation of the Whig party, but it has certainly had its influence on such important studies as Gabor S. Boritt's *Lincoln and the Economics of the American Dream* (1978). And "The Radicals and Lincoln" has stimulated supporters and critics to produce a veritable library of books and articles.

In this new edition I have rearranged the essays, so that they appear in a more logical order, with the new essays interspersed at the appropriate points. I was tempted to make extensive revisions in the older essays, so as to bring them up to date. For instance, just a few paragraphs added to "Getting Right with Lincoln" would tell how all the presidential candidates in the 2000 election invoked Lincoln's blessing, and I longed to include Governor Jesse Ventura's announcement that he had much in common with Abraham Lincoln since they were both wrestlers. But such rewriting would double the size of this little book. On the whole it has seemed best to let the essays stand as originally written (with minor corrections of facts and typographical errors), but I have updated the bibliographical essays.

I hope that this new edition will continue to provide interest and controversy. My objective, as always, has been to keep Civil War studies, and especially accounts of Abraham Lincoln, from degenerating into antiquarianism by asking fresh questions and by suggesting fresh answers to old questions. Because these essays represent an effort to think about Lincoln and the Civil War in a different way, they are, to some extent, experimental efforts. I have no doubt at times fallen into errors of fact or interpretation, and, like most innovators, I may have stated ideas too baldly. I regret these weaknesses, but I do not apologize for my belief that the Civil War era is the most fascinating period in American history. It ought to attract our best minds and our most imaginative writers.

David Herbert Donald

LINCOLN

RECONSIDERED

ONE

Getting Right with Lincoln

I

ABOUT NO OTHER AMERICAN have so many words been written as about Abraham Lincoln. Jay Monaghan's *Lincoln Bibliography* requires 1,079 pages merely to list the books and pamphlets published before 1939, when even the experts lost count. On library shelves the multivolumed biographies by Nicolay and Hay, Sandburg, and Randall and Current stand cover to cover with *Lincoln Never Smoked a Cigarette* and *Abraham Lincoln on the Coming of the Caterpillar Tractor.* Every February sees a fresh flood of Lincoln Day oratory and verse.

This extraordinary interest in the details of Lincoln's life seems the more astonishing in light of his low contemporary standing. His associates were sure there were greater figures in their era; usually they had at least one such person in mind—and close at home at that. Lincoln they thought a simple Susan, a baboon, an aimless punster, a smutty joker. He left the highway of principle to pursue the devious paths of expediency. A "huckster in politics," sneered Wendell Phillips, "a first-rate *second-rate* man." A Springfield neighbor called him "The craftiest and *most dishonest politician that ever disgraced an office in America.*" "If I wanted to paint a despot, a man perfectly regardless of every constitutional right of the people," cried Saulsbury of Delaware in the Senate, "I would paint the hideous form of Abraham Lincoln. . . ."

Not even assassination at once translated Lincoln into saint-hood. "The decease of Mr. Lincoln is a great national bereave-ment," conceded Representative J. M. Ashley of Ohio, "but I am not so sure it is so much of a national loss." Within eight hours of his murder Republican Congressmen in secret caucus agreed that "his death is a godsend to our cause." Andrew Johnson, they believed, would carry through the proposed social revolution in the South that the conciliatory Lincoln had blocked. Now, crowed Ben Wade, "there will be no trouble running the government."

But politicians of all parties were apparently startled by the extent of the national grief over Lincoln, and, politicanlike, they decided to capitalize upon it. Democrats were, of course, under a handicap, but a surprising number of them now discovered that they had really heartily endorsed the Lincoln program. That vicious Copperhead sheet the Chicago *Times* discerned "indica-tions of the last few days of [Lincoln's] life that he might command [Democratic] support on the close of the war," and Clement L. Val-landigham reported that even the peace men had begun "to turn toward Lincoln for deliverance."

The Republicans' claim to Lincoln was surely somewhat more plausible, and, being in a majority in Congress, they were able to make it good by staging a three-week funeral procession, witnessed by millions of persons, in which Lincoln's body was dragged by spe-cial train, to the accompaniment of mourning bells and wailing choirs, through the principal cities of the North. Democrat Charles Mason of Iowa though the whole affair a political trick, like the "crafty skill of Mark Anthony [*sic*] in displaying to the Roman peo-ple the bloody mantle of Caesar." Republican Radicals, he felt, in seeking a vindictive peace and a new social order for the South, wanted "to make . . . political capital out of the murder. They wish to strengthen their hands and brutalize the hearts of the Northern people till there shall be general concurrence in all measures of confiscation and extermination. . . ."

That was precisely what the Radicals intended and did. Their Lincoln eulogies were carefully directed toward proving that Democrats had been in part responsible for Lincoln's death and toward demonstrating that Negro suffrage was necessary in order to prevent the traitors from returning to power. In his Lincoln oration in Boston, Charles Sumner, theorist for the Radical faction, carefully interjected a strong plea for Negro enfranchisement, which his party friends found "very *cunning.*"

Meanwhile, a third contender for the Lincolnian mantle appeared in the person of Andrew Johnson, the new President. After a momentary aberration in which he seemed more radical than the Radicals, Johnson adopted a conciliatory policy toward the South, granting general amnesty and exacting neither confiscation of property nor Negro suffrage. All this in the eyes of the Radicals was bad enough, but he did it all in the name of Lincoln. William H. Seward, who continued as Secretary of State, assured all comers that the Johnson reconstruction plans "grew during the administration of Mr. Lincoln," and in his proclamations setting up provisional governments in the South, the President specifically referred to Lincoln's earlier actions as his precedents.

Republican Radicals were furious. Johnson they considered a traitor, all the more dangerous because he threatened to divert the idolization of Lincoln, so carefully fostered by the Radicals, into support of an antiradical program. "Is there no way to arrest the insane course of the President . . . ?" groaned Thaddeus Stevens.

There was a way, and it is not too much of an oversimplification to regard the ensuing struggle between President and Congress as a ghoulish tugging at Lincoln's shroud; both parties needed to identify Lincoln with their respective reconstruction programs. It was a vindictive quarrel, and shrill denunciation by the one faction provoked harsher abuse from the other. Johnson, publicly branding Sumner, Stevens, and Wendell Phillips as "opposed to the fundamental principles of this government," asked petulantly: "Are [they] . . . not satisfied . . . with one martyr? Does not the blood of Lincoln appease [their] . . . vengeance and wrath . . . ?" And Ben Butler, speaking for the Radicals thus accused, replied by impeaching the President before the Senate: "By murder most foul . . . [Johnson] succeeded to the Presidency, and is the elect of an assassin to that high office. . . ." In the Republican national convention

5

of 1868 it was openly charged that "the treachery of Andrew Johnson . . . cost us the life of Abraham Lincoln."

The rival parties of the Reconstruction era were not, of course, historians quibbling over a footnote. They were politicians seeking power, and they invoked Lincoln's name to win votes. Among the Negroes of the South they knew that identification with Lincoln might assure a candidate of victory. In Lexington, South Carolina, for instance, the fall elections of 1867 were expected to be close, and Radicals felt that they must carry the entire Negro vote. Proudly the ward heeler wrote Charles Sumner of their methods. The Republicans secretly printed their own ballots, to be distributed on the day of the election, which "were to contain a *sign* . . . and *by it*, we hoped to conquer." "I inclose a ticket," he continued, "and you will see the sign—no less than Abraham Lincoln, the martyr to Liberty—and no colored man dared refuse it—nor did one single one fail to vote it. . . . When our ticket distributers . . . showed their tickets with the face of Lincoln, their eyes beamed with gratitude, and one old worn out freedman exclaimed 'Tank God, I tought he would send you to us!' "

In the Northern states Republican use of the Lincoln symbol was somewhat more literate but scarcely less emotional. During the campaign of 1868, Edwin M. Stanton, whose conversion to Lincolnian views might be termed posthumous, swept his Pennsylvania audiences for Grant by reading the Gettysburg address. Then he said, tearfully: "That is the voice of God speaking through the lips of Abraham Lincoln! . . . You hear the voice of Father Abraham here tonight. Did he die in vain? . . . Let us here, every one, with uplifted hand, declare before Almighty God that the precious gift of this great heritage, consecrated in the blood of our soldiers, shall never perish from the earth. Now—" and he uplifted his hands— "all hands to God. I SWEAR IT!" After which his auditors all presumably went out and voted Republican.

II

AFTER JOHNSON WAS DEFEATED, it seemed to be Lincoln and the Republican party, one and inseparable. Other parties, of course, could revere and admire Lincoln as a great American, but it was clear to the right-thinking that the Great Martyr was Republican property. In periodic campaign addresses Republicans invoked the Great Emancipator to bless the good cause and to smite the unrighteous. To some these terms might need definition, but not to Republicans. Lincoln, they were sure, would favor the high tariff; urge the annexation of the Philippines; oppose greenbackism, socialism, populism, and labor unions; fight the income tax; and assail the League of Nations and the World Court.

Every four years Republican hopefuls sought—and presumably secured—Lincoln's endorsement. According to the campaign literature, Lincoln invariably bore marked physical or moral resemblance to the party's candidates, including such unlikely persons as William McKinley, William Howard Taft, and Calvin Coolidge. Year after year Republican politicos reviewed their party's lineage in Lincoln Day addresses that the world has little noted nor long remembered. One oration, however, deserves to be treasured—that of Warren G. Harding, commencing: "Destiny made Lincoln the agency of fulfillment, held the inherited covenant inviolate and gave him to the ages. No words can magnify or worship glorify." As W. S. Gilbert observes, "The meaning doesn't matter if it's only idle chatter of a transcendental kind."

The Lincoln cult in literature was closely connected with this party tradition. The laudatory Lincoln biographies—those of Holland, Nicolay and Hay, and the like—were written by men who firmly believed that, next to the dog, the Republican party was man's best friend. Orated George S. Boutwell, somewhat inaccurately: "The Republican Party gave to Mr. Lincoln the opportunity on which his fame rests, and his fame is the inheritance of the Republican party. . . . When we set forth the character and services

7

of Mr. Lincoln we set forth as well the claims of the Republican party to the gratitude and confidence of the country. . . ."

Not until 1887 did the party formally begin holding annual rallies on February 12. By that time the outlines of the Lincoln portrait were fading in even the most tenacious Republican memory and a yearly banquet offered the dual opportunity to retouch the portrait and to refill the party treasury. This useful custom rapidly spread, and today most major Republican congregations hold dinners on Lincoln's birthday. Every year these somewhat grim rites of early spring are reported in the newspapers, and drearier reading would be hard to find. Take, for instance, the seventeenth annual Lincoln Day dinner of the New York Republican Club, held at the Waldorf-Astoria in 1903. Some five hundred men attended—their wives were segregated in those happy, bygone days—and ate the seven-course dinner. As the menu was in French, Lincoln probably could not have known what was served; and as the food, as is usual at banquets, was reported atrocious, he perhaps would not have wished to. Later the "handsomely gowned" women were permitted to join their spouses, electricity illuminated the figure of an elephant behind the speakers' table, and Lincoln's spirit was invoked to be present. The presiding officer read regrets from dignitaries unable to attend—Senators, Supreme Court Justices, party bigwigs. President Theodore Roosevelt wrote: "I feel that not merely the Republican Party, but all believers in the country, should do everything in their power to keep alive the memory of Abraham Lincoln." That was about the only nonpartisan note of the evening.

There followed—as always—addresses. The chief speaker was former Governor Frank S. Black of New York, chosen for his alleged resemblance to Lincoln. "There are subjects," he began, "upon which nothing new can be said"—but this did not deter him from continuing. His theme was the advantage of Lincoln's poverty. "The child may shiver in the fury of the blast which no maternal tenderness can shield him from, but he may feel a helpless tear drop upon his cheek which will keep him warm till the snows of time have covered his hair." His well-clad auditors, safe from the wintry blast, applauded. "It is not wealth that counts in the making of the world, but character. . . . Give me the hut that is small enough, the poverty that is deep enough, the love that is great enough, and I will raise from them the best there is in human character." Again his hearers, who, after all, were considerably poorer for their attendance at this gathering, applauded the virtues of poverty.

After some minutes—a good many minutes—more of this, a Vermont judge spoke on Lincoln and Wendell Phillips. Then Congressman Cushman of Washington followed on "Abraham Lincoln and the Northwest," concluding: "And with no sordid thought of gain for myself or for my party, I say that it beats in every throb of my heart tonight that the greatest good, the grandest future, and the most immortal destiny of our nation lies [*sic*] with the Republican Party." Another Congressman then talked about "Lincoln's War Secretary," but his remarks have fortunately not been preserved. Late at night, in various stages of numbness the guests escaped, clutching their sacred relics of the reincarnation they had just witnessed— watch fobs showing Lincoln swinging a woodman's mallet.

III

For decades the Republican claim to Lincoln so repeatedly asserted went virtually unquestioned. Although minor parties from time to time jeered that a McKinley or a Coolidge had hardly the physique for a rail-splitter, Democrats for the most part respected the Republican title. Grover Cleveland, for instance, making a tour of the Middle West in 1887, carefully avoided a stop at Springfield, Illinois, not because he lacked admiration for Lincoln but because he felt that the Lincoln shrines were Republican preserves. Woodrow Wilson did make Lincoln Day speeches— and to Democrats, at that—but he admitted the prior Republican claim by beginning: "I sometimes think it a singular circumstance that the present Republican party should have sprung from Lincoln, but that is one of the mysteries of Providence. . . ."

In 1912, however, Lincoln became a partisan issue. Denying any wish to "treat [Lincoln's] name as a mere party symbol," President

Taft claimed Lincoln as a regular who would never ally himself with Theodore Roosevelt's Progressives. "Lincoln knew no such word as insurgent," former Congressman Charles F. Scott echoed his chief, "for it never entered his mind to consider himself more important than his principles." But Theodore Roosevelt insisted that Lincoln was on his side: "The official leaders of the Republican party today are the spiritual heirs of the men who warred against Lincoln, who railed at him as a revolutionist, . . . who accused him of being a radical, an innovator, an opponent of the Constitution and an enemy of property." By 1916, however, in Lincoln's name, Roosevelt urged his Progressive following to return to the regular party ranks; Lincoln had come home.

It was not until 1932 that another serious effort was made to raid the Republican closet and steal the stovepipe hat. Harassed Herbert Hoover, making the traditional pilgrimage to Springfield, likened himself to Lincoln in the dark days of 1864, and found victory over the Depression just a matter of fighting it out on this line if it took all summer. Traditionally, Democrats had regarded such oratory as an exclusively Republican prerogative, but now a new spirit had entered that party. James A. Farley piously announced himself "shocked" at Hoover's partisan use of the Lincoln symbol, and Gifford Pinchot declared that Lincoln in these sad days "would not get to first base" with the Republican party on "his platform of human rights." It was even suggested that campaigning Governor Franklin Roosevelt might make an address at Lincoln's tomb, a report that caused cries of "sacrilege" among Springfield Republicans, one of whom threatened an injunction to stop this Democratic outrage.

Mr. Roosevelt did not then speak as Lincoln's successor, but he was very shortly to assume the mantle of the Great Emancipator. In fact, he seemed to rummage through the clothes closet of American history and take his pick of garments. He understood what was meant by "the usable past." The notion that Lincoln was a Republican, President Roosevelt dismissed as an idea as outmoded as the horse and buggy, the balanced budget, and the nine-man Supreme Court. His was the new interpretation of history. "Does anyone maintain that the Republican party from 1868 to 1938 (with the possible exception of a few years under Theodore Roosevelt) was the party of Abraham Lincoln?" he queried. Lincoln he named along with Jefferson and Jackson and Wilson (Henry Wallace was to add the prophet Amos and the Boston Tea Party mob) as a father of the New Deal.

Repeatedly the New Dealers urged their claim to the Lincoln tradition. Mayor Fiorello La Guardia was positive that present-day Republicans "have nothing in common" with Lincoln. Quite the contrary. Was it not Lincoln who said "the legitimate object of government is to do for a community of people whatever they need to have done, but cannot do for themselves, in their separate and individual capacities"? Mr. Roosevelt was so taken with this apparent justification of the New Deal's economic policies that he quoted the statement on at least three occasions. On specific issues Democrats cited Lincoln with devastating effectiveness. Republicans who reacted with horror to President Roosevelt's denunciation of the Supreme Court were reminded by Attorney General Homer Cummings that Lincoln had attacked the Court's Dred Scott decision, and when Mr. Roosevelt defended his court-packing scheme, he observed that Lincoln also had increased the number of Supreme Court justices.

Not surprisingly, most Republicans were irate at this Democratic effort to get in on their act. Very few would agree with Wendell Willkie, who deplored all partisan use of national heroes and in effect urged an armistice. ". . . Neither Mr. Roosevelt nor I myself are great men," he observed, in what was undoubtedly one of the worst guesses in recent history. "Neither of us has demonstrated any of the qualities of greatness . . . [of] Washington or Lincoln. . . . Therefore, in the discussions of an issue of a campaign, . . . it will do us no good to draw these historical illusions." (The printer spelled it so—a Democrat, no doubt) "The question is . . . What does he believe, and what do I believe?"

But most Republicans were not so willing to surrender their political treasure. The New Deal's claim to Lincoln was a dirty

Roosevelt trick, they snarled. Year after year, during the dark New Deal days, Republicans continued to rally on Lincoln's birthday, and they "sacrificed thousands of banquet chickens to the memory of their patron saint and their speakers said Roosevelt was becoming a dictator." In 1939, for instance, Herbert Hoover was willingly recalled from an unwilling retirement to address the Waldorf-Astoria dinner and to rebuke the Democrats for riding on the Republican range. "Whatever this New Deal system is," the ex-President snapped, "it is certain that it did not come from Abraham Lincoln." Other Republicans were positive that Lincoln would oppose the high income tax, social security, the court-reorganization scheme, aid to Britain, and a third term. Lincoln would especially have detested the un-Americanism of the New Deal, declared Colonel Robert R. McCormick of the Chicago *Tribune*. "Dictatorship threatens to engulf the liberties of the American people," the Colonel darkly warned. "A band of conspirators including one Felix Frankfurter, like Adolf Hitler, born an Austrian, impregnated with the historic doctrine of Austrian absolutism, plans to inflict this Oriental atrocity upon our Republican people. The Congress of the United States has been corrupted with bribes. . . . Four billion eight hundred million dollars . . . has been appropriated to corrupt the electors. The unscrupulous . . . Jim Farley is at work behind the smiling mask of Franklin Roosevelt to bring the end of self-government in the world. . . . In this grave moment, I recall to you these words of Abraham Lincoln. . . ."

IV

DESPITE THESE PLAINTIVE EFFORTS to reclaim him, Lincoln was by now everybody's grandfather. No reputable political organization could omit a reference to the Great Emancipator, nor could the disreputable ones. The Communist party began holding Lincoln-Lenin rallies in February, and the party headquarters in New York were adorned with Lincoln's photographs. Neither the "Republican-Liberty League-Hearst combination" nor the Democratic party, "whose main base in the reactionary Solid South," was the legitimate heir of Lincoln, claimed Earl Browder. "The times call again for a Lincoln, for a new party, for a new program." At the same time that he was a Communist, Lincoln was also a vegetarian, a socialist, a prohibitionist, a greenbacker, and a proponent of Union Now.

In the 1948 election, everybody was for Lincoln. Dixiecrats remembered that Lincoln, as a fellow Southerner, preferred letting the race problem work itself out. Henry Wallace's Progressives asserted that they were heirs of Jefferson, Jackson, *and* Lincoln. Thomas E. Dewey, according to his running-mate, bore a striking resemblance to Lincoln—spiritual rather than physical, one judges—and President Truman claimed that if Lincoln were alive, he would be a Democrat. Finally Lincoln has become a nonpartisan, nonsectional hero. It seems, as Congressman Everett Dirksen solemnly assured his Republican colleagues, that these days the first task of a politician is "to get right with . . . Lincoln."

Obviously all this ballyhoo has had something to do with the continually growing Lincoln legend, but it alone is not sufficient explanation. Other party greats have been cited and discarded. It is difficult to imagine anyone in the 1950's asking: "What would Charles Sumner do if he were here today?" One reason is that it is perfectly simple to ascertain what Sumner would do. Perhaps the secret of Lincoln's continuing vogue is his essential ambiguity. He can be cited on all sides of all questions.

A moralist may deplore Lincoln's noncommittal attitude, but it should be remembered that this fundamental opportunism is characteristic of major American political leaders from Jefferson to Franklin D. Roosevelt. Our great presidents have joyously played the political piano by ear, making up the melody as they went. At only one time have rigid ideologists dominated our national government—the Sumners of the North, the Jefferson Davises of the South—and the result was near disaster. Today, badly frightened if well-intentioned citizens are calling upon historians and teachers to draw up a rigid credo for Americanism, to teach "American values." To do so is to forget Lincoln's nonideological approach. In our age of anxiety it is pertinent to remember that our most enduring political symbolism derives from Lincoln, whose one dogma was an absence of dogma.

TWO

The Folklore Lincoln

I

THE LINCOLN CULT IS ALMOST an American religion. It has its high priests in the form of Lincoln "authorities" and its worshippers in the thousands of "fans" who think, talk, and read Lincoln every day. The very name of its founder possesses magical significance—witness its use in advertising everything from automobiles to barbershops. In many states his birthday became a holiday, commemorated with solemn ceremonies. In 1909, the centennial of his birth, Illinois teachers were directed to devote at least half of the day of February 12 to "public exercises . . . patriotic music, recitations of sayings and verses . . . and speeches." The schoolchildren were to conclude the celebration by chanting in unison, with their faces turned toward Springfield, the following ritual:

> A blend of mirth and sadness, smiles and tears;
> A quaint knight errant of the pioneers;
> A homely hero, born of star and sod;
> A Peasant Prince; a masterpiece of God.

The Lincoln birthplace in Kentucky, the memorial in Washington, and the tomb in Illinois have become national shrines visited by thousands each week.

It was probably inevitable that Lincoln should have, as Emerson said, "become mythological in a very few years." America was badly in need of a hero. By 1865 George Washington seemed so dignified and remote that it was hard to think of him as a man, much less as a boy; he was a portrait by Peale or a Houdon bust. Davy Crockett had degenerated from frontier hero into comic legend. Andrew Jackson, Henry Clay, and Daniel Webster were already slipping into the limbo of lost souls, the history books.

The times and events of the Civil War had made a great popular leader necessary. There had been the emotional strain of war, the taut peril of defeat, the thrill of battles won, the release of peace. Then had come the calamitous, disastrous assassination. The people's grief was immediate and it was immense. Properly to describe it one would need the eloquence of a Whitman or a Sandburg. Men had a lost feeling. "The news of his going," mourned William H. Herndon, "struck me dumb, the deed being so infernally wicked . . . so huge in consequences, that it was too large to enter my brain. Hence it was incomprehensible, leaving a misty distant doubt of its truth. It *yet* does not appear like a worldly reality."

Mourning intensified grief. The trappings of death—the black-draped catafalque, the silent train that moved by a circuitous route over the land, the white-robed choirs that wailed a dirge, the crepe-veiled women, the stone-faced men—made Lincoln's passing seem even more calamitous. Over a million persons took a last sad look at the face in the casket and went away treasuring an unforgettable memory. They became of that select group who had seen Lincoln plain.

II

IN THOSE DARK POSTWAR DECADES there was keen interest in the Great Emancipator and Great Martyr—those two phrases, always in capitals, keep cropping up in nearly all the correspondence of the period. There were those who speculated on what Lincoln would have done had he lived, and there were more who tried to recall what he had done while alive. An avid audience looked forward eagerly to the memoirs and reminiscences that began to flood the country. Jay Monaghan's *Lincoln Biography* lists over four hundred and fifty speeches, sermons, and histories of Lincoln that appeared in the year of his death.

To this urgent demand for details on Lincoln's life, few would answer as did George Spears, a friend from New Salem days, who explained the brevity of his recollections by declaring: "At that time I had no idea of his ever being President therefore I did not notice his course as close as I should of." Not only persons who knew Lincoln retailed "facts" to the eager world, but also those who had merely met the President, or those who thought they had met him, or those who wished to have met him. Stories, sometimes without the slightest shadow of factual foundation, were spread by word of mouth, and by mere repetition gained authenticity. Then they appeared in Lincoln biographies and have been handed down ever since as indubitably accurate.

At the time of Lincoln's death there was no single pattern into which the stories and anecdotes about him could fit. In the blurred memories of former slaves there was the shadowy outline of a preternaturally shrewd Lincoln, half Moses, half Yankee. "I think Abe Lincoln was next to the Lord," said one ex-slave. "He done all he could for the slaves; he set 'em free." Then the aged Negro went on to "reminisce":

'Fore the election he [Lincoln] traveled all over the South, and he come to our house and slept in Old Mistress' bed. Didn't nobody know who he was. . . . He come to our house and he watched close. . . . When he got back up North he writ Old Master a letter and told him that he was going to have to free his slaves, that everybody was going to have to. . . . He also told him that he had visited at his house and if he doubted it to go in the room he slept in and look on the bedstead at the head and he'd see where he'd writ his name. Sure enough, there was his name: A. Lincoln.

Gradually the Negro built up a more emotional image of Lincoln, a perfect man and, in a peculiarly individual way, a personal emancipator. In Negro houses all over the nation one could find "many old pictures of Lincoln pasted on the walls of the sitting room over the mantelpiece. . . . They just had to have Lincoln near them," explains their chronicler, John E. Washington; "they loved him so." "His life to these humble people was a miracle, and his memory has become a benediction," Dr. Washington adds. "To the deeply emotional and religious slave, Lincoln was an earthly incarnation of the Savior of mankind."

At the other extreme were the stories spread by Lincoln's political enemies, legends that still persist in some parts of the South. To these the sixteenth President was only "a man of coarse nature, a self-seeking politician, who craved high office . . . to satisfy his own burning desire for distinction." ". . . his real name is Abraham Hanks," one political opponent charged. "He is the illegitimate son by an [sic] man named Inlow—from a Negress named Hanna Hanks." His presumptive parents were immoral, shiftless poor white trash. Unscrupulous as a lawyer, he was unprincipled as a politician. He was a man of low morality, and his "inordinate love of the lascivious, of smut," it was whispered, was "something nearly akin to lunacy."

III

NATURALLY, the strongest growth of Lincoln legends has occurred in the North. There have been, in general, two opposing schools of tradition. One, essentially literary in character and often of New England or Eastern sponsorship, presented a prettified Lincoln, a combination of George Washington and Christ. Occasionally there were difficulties in reconciling the two ideas, and the resulting portrait looks somewhat like a Gilbert Stuart painting with a halo dubbed in by later, less skillful hands. The problem was to reconcile the standards of democracy in the gilded age with the familiar pattern of the Christ story. Fortunately for authors, consistency is not an essential in folklore.

In eulogies, sermons, birthday speeches, Republican campaign addresses, orations before the G.A.R., and in poems too numerous to count and too tedious to read, one gets a glimpse of the pattern. This Lincoln has the outlines of a mythological hero; he is a demigod. Born in obscure circumstances, he rose over hardships, became President, was lawgiver to the Negro people, won a tremendous victory, and was killed at the height of his power. By his death he expiated the sins of his country. After one makes the obvious concessions required by mid-century morality and by the exigencies of a republican form of government, this Lincoln conforms very closely to the type of ideal hero in classical mythology.

The eulogists had some doubts as to how Lincoln's ancestry should be presented. A mythological hero should spring from unknown parentage (or at least it is concealed even from himself), sent by the gods to save his tribe. There are a number of Lincoln poets and biographers who ask: "Whence came this man?" and answer: "As if on the wings of the winds of God that blew!" On the other hand, it comported more with American notions of respectability that the hero should have at least some family connections. The Lincolns have, therefore, been traced in elaborate monographs back to the early Massachusetts settlers and even to the English family of that name. The Hankses have been "proved" to derive their name from an Egyptian dynasty, or, as an alternative explanation, they were relatives of the Lees of Virginia.

Regardless of origins, the biographers were sure of one thing. Lincoln loved his angel-mother. It is characteristic of the American attitude toward family life and of the extreme veneration for the maternal principle that the utterly unknown Nancy Hanks should be described as "a whole-hearted Christian," "a woman of marked natural abilities," of "strong mental powers and deep-toned piety," whose rigid observance of the Sabbath became a byword in frontier Kentucky—in short, "a remarkable woman." "A great man," asserted J. G. Holland in his widely circulated *Life of Abraham Lin-*

coln, "never drew his infant life from a purer or more womanly bosom than her own; and Mr. Lincoln always looked back to her with an unspeakable affection."

Lincoln's early life became, to this school of biography, an illustration of how determination and energy could triumph over circumstances; this Lincoln was the transcendent rail-splitter. It was a carefully manipulated symbolism that had begun at the Illinois state Republican convention of 1860 when rails that Lincoln might have split were introduced to elicit applause. The theme was drummed and piped and bugled all through the campaigns of 1860 and 1864, and the tale of Lincoln's "life of labor" that "brought forth his kingly qualities of soul" has become a part of the American tradition. Lincoln was never to escape; his Civil War administration would be appraised in terms of his early struggles:

> *Out yonder splitting rails his mind had fed*
> *On Freedom — now he put her foes to rout.*

From these origins he rose to become President of the United States, and, surprisingly enough, a successful President. There must have been, a great many people believed, some supernatural force, some divine guidance behind his rise. "Out of the unknown, and by ways that even he knew not," orated one centennial speaker, becoming more mystical with each phrase, "came to this place of power, Abraham Lincoln. He came mysteriously chosen . . . by the instinctive voice of a predestined people. Called because he was chosen; chosen, because he was already choice."

There were elements in Lincoln's personality and career that did not blend well in this portrait of a demigod. He was indubitably homely — not a major difficulty, to be sure, yet if a hero is not handsome he should at least be impressive. Rhymesters went to great length to explain the truth. Was Lincoln "ungainly, plain"? Not at all. "Grave was his visage," it was admitted, "but no cloud could dull the radiance from within that made it beautiful." A more serious obstacle was Lincoln's levity. He told jokes — a thing unprecedented in the record of mythology. Writers were more familiar with the idea of "one who knew not play, nor ever tasted rest." How could a man of sadness and tears laugh at Artemus Ward? One poet suggested that Lincoln's laughter was really a sort of anodyne "to cease his ceaseless dole." Thus Lincoln became the laughing man of sorrows.

Another difficulty was Lincoln's religion. It was embarrassing that this "soldier of his Captain Christ" belonged to no Christian church. Shortly after Lincoln's death there began to appear a veritable flood of affidavits and statements to prove, as Holland put it, that "Lincoln's power" had been the "power of a true-hearted Christian man." Reminiscences on this point probably include more nonsense than can be found anywhere else in the whole tiresome mass of spurious Lincoln recollections. To him are attributed the most improbable statements. Lincoln was supposed to have had a secret conference with Newton Bateman, Illinois superintendent of public instruction, during which he pulled a Testament from his bosom and pointed to it as *"this rock* on which I stand." "I know," he is alleged to have confided, "that liberty is right, for Christ teaches it and Christ is God."

Countless similar statements were given wide newspaper circulation. Lincoln reportedly ran upon one Benjamin B. Smith, a minister of Canton, Missouri, in a railway station, brought him into his office, and begged from the willing pastor a private, hour-long discourse upon "foreordination, election and predestination." During the darkest hours of the war Lincoln was supposed to have left his post in Washington in order to pray with Henry Ward Beecher in Brooklyn. So it went. There were those who could demonstrate that Lincoln was a Catholic, a Congregationalist, a Methodist, a Presbyterian, a Universalist, or a Spiritualist. Conflicting claims became so amusing that the editor of the Springfield *Illinois State Register* rejected them as "all wrong." "We are," he remarked whimsically, "prepared to prove by indisputable documentary evidence that he was a Mormon, and the boon companion of Joe Smith."

For these minor defects Lincoln amply compensated by the manner of his passing. His assassination at once brought to mind the tender, familiar outlines of the Christ story. Lincoln as "Savior of his country" was by his death expiating the sins of the nation. The idea had universal appeal. One has only to leaf through the pages of Lloyd Lewis's *Myths after Lincoln* to discover how frequently the idea of vicarious sacrifice recurred to Northern preachers on that dread Black Easter of 1865. Some pointed to the significance of Lincoln's martyrdom on Good Friday. "It is no blasphemy against the Son of God," asserted a Connecticut parson, "that we declare the fitness of the slaying of the second Father of our Republic on the anniversary of the day on which He was slain. Jesus Christ died for the world, Abraham Lincoln died for his country." Even so early the pattern of apotheosis was complete. America had a martyr hero, a perfect man, born to do great things, pure in heart, noble in action, and constant in principle. This was Lincoln, "President, savior of the republic, emancipator of a race, true Christian, true man."

IV

LINCOLN WAS SAVED from this kind of deification by a different stream of tradition, frequently Western in origin and more truly folkloristic in quality. The grotesque hero—the Gargantua or the Till Eulenspiegel—is one of the oldest and most familiar patterns in folk literature. In America the type had been already exemplified by such favorites as Davy Crockett, Mike Fink, and Paul Bunyan. Of a like cut was the myth of Lincoln as frontier hero. This Lincoln of "folk say" was the practical joker, the teller of tall and lusty tales. Stupendously strong, he was also marvelously lazy. A true romantic, he pined over the grave of Ann Rutledge, but he also lampooned one woman who refused him and jilted another who accepted. He was Old Abe, a Westerner, and his long flapping arms were not the wings of an angel.

This folk pattern of Lincoln as frontier hero had been sketched in outline before his death. After his assassination the details were filled in. Many of the stories in the strong Western tradition can be traced back to Herndon, Lincoln's law partner, who has been called the "master myth-maker" of Lincoln folklore. Herndon did not invent the legends, but his singular personality made him peculiarly receptive to this type of Western mythology. Herndon was born in Kentucky, and as an early German traveler put it, "the Kentuckian is a peculiar man." Moody, erratic, loquacious, addicted to high-flown "philosophical" language, but with a fondness for earthy stories, Herndon had shortly after his partner's death decided to write a biography of Lincoln. From the very outset he had in mind showing Lincoln as a Western character, shaped by the "power of mud, flowers, & mind" which he had encountered in the pioneer Northwest. Deliberately he sought to emphasize those factors which would distinguish Lincoln as a Westerner from his Eastern contemporaries. He proposed to exhibit "the type" of the "original western and south-western pioneer— . . . at times . . . somewhat open, candid, sincere, energetic, spontaneous, trusting, tolerant, brave and generous."

Seeking information about Lincoln, Herndon interviewed older settlers in central Illinois and southern Indiana at just the time when the outlines of the folk portrait were becoming firmly established. From his notes emerged a folkloristic picture of a semi-legendary frontier hero. The stories Herndon collected fall into patterns familiar to the student of American folklore. Some remembered Lincoln as a ring-tailed roarer of the Davy Crockett type, who would wave a whisky bottle over his head to drive back his foes, shouting that "he was the big buck at the lick." There were tales of the Paul Bunyan variety, describing how Lincoln would "frequently take a barrel of whisky by the chimes and lift it up to his face as if to drink out of the bung-hole," a feat that "he could accomplish with greatest ease."

This was the Lincoln who chastely wooed Ann Rutledge and, when she died, pined sadly over her grave. "My heart," he was supposed to have said, "lies buried there." More in the frontier tradition was his courtship of Mary Owens, a well-educated Kentucky lady who refused his hand. Afterward Lincoln described her as "weather-beaten," "oversize," and lacking teeth. Of a like pattern were the tales Herndon accumulated of Lincoln's domestic unhappiness with Mary Todd, for the henpecked husband is one of the oldest comic types and was a favorite in the Western joke books of the day. Herndon also collected irreligious or, as he called them, "infidel" statements attributed to Lincoln; the folk hero is frequently anticlerical.

Many of these tales probably had a grain of historical truth, and their evolution exhibits the familiar developments of folk literature. "If a man has been well known for special powers," Robert Price has pointed out in his examination of the Johnny Appleseed traditions, "folk fancies soon seize upon particular instances of these powers, begin to enhance them into facts of remarkable quality, and then proceed, as the desire for greater color grows, to invent still others that will markedly emphasize the quality admired." As the historical personage becomes absorbed in the myth, "the whole cycle of his birth, youth, education, loves, mating, maturity, and death becomes significant and grows increasingly in color and particular detail." On a rather sophisticated plane, the Lincoln of Western legend represented a true folk-hero type.

The folkloristic quality of these stories is sometimes overlooked. When Herndon visited in Indiana, he was told of verses that Lincoln had written to celebrate the wedding of his sister:

> *When Adam was created*
> *He dwelt in Eden's shade,*
> *As Moses has recorded,*
> *And soon a bride was made.*

(The poem continues for seven additional stanzas.) Dr. Milo M. Quaife has traced this ballad back to early English folk verse and has shown that it was introduced into America before the Revolutionary War. In the process of being handed down, it somehow became identified in the minds of backwoods Hoosiers with Lincoln; it was related to Herndon as such; he published the verses in his Lincoln biography; and the poem is not infrequently cited as Lincoln's original composition. Of the making of myths there is no end.

The process of evolving Western legends about Lincoln neither began nor ended with Herndon. Gossip, imagination, delayed recollection, and hearsay have all continued to multiply "Lincoln" stories. Sometimes the results of this accumulation of "folk say" are amusing. One can take, for example, a less familiar episode in Lincoln's early career—his projected duel with James Shields. The actual facts of the affair are easily ascertained. In 1842 Mary Todd and Julia Jayne published anonymously in the *Sangamo Journal* some satirical verses about Shields, then Illinois state auditor. That hot-tempered Irishman demanded of the editor the names of the writers, and Lincoln, to protect the ladies, offered to take the blame. After some stilted correspondence and much dashing back and forth of seconds, a duel with broadswords was arranged. Ultimately, however, explanations and apologies were made, and actual combat was averted. The affair remained a sore memory to Lincoln, and he disliked hearing the episode referred to. The whole affair is summarized in any good Lincoln biography.

As this same tale comes down in folklore, the whole emphasis is altered. It becomes an illustration of Lincoln the humorist and the practical joker. The duel had an amusing origin, according to one old settler who had heard another old-timer tell the story:

> Lawyer Shields and Julia Jayne were seated together at the supper table. Across the table from them sat Abe and Mary Todd. By and by the lawyer squeezed Julia's hand. In those days, you know, a pin was a woman's weapon. Julia used it when Shields squeezed her hand. And that made him scream. . . . Lincoln, who was a laughing fellow, hawhawed right out loud, much to the embarrassment of Shields. Well to make a long story short, Shield[s] issued a duel challenge to Abe.

Another version gives a play-by-play account of the duel that never happened. "Shields fired and missed," says this "eyewitness," speaking of an encounter that was to have been fought with broadswords.

"Lincoln then took steady aim and fired. A blotch of read [sic] appeared on the breast of Shields who fell to the ground thinking he was mortally wounded, but in fact was unhurt. Lincoln's gun was loaded with pokeberries."

To treat such statements simply as exaggerated reminiscences is to miss their significance. They are really folk stories. Seldom do they have an identifiable author, for the narrator is recounting what "they said." The very pattern of the statement is significant; "to make a long story short" is a frequent formula to conclude a folk tale. The Shields episode is only one less widely known incident about which a surprisingly large amount of folklore has accumulated. The body of tradition concerning Lincoln's courtship, his marriage, or his law practice is much more voluminous. And there is an extensive cycle of ribald and Rabelaisian stories attributed to Lincoln, for the most part unprintable and now almost forgotten.

V

FEW NEGROES have written books about their great emancipator, and the viciously anti-Lincoln publications are nearly forgotten, but the other two major currents of tradition have produced a mountainous pile of Lincoln literature. Writers who fitted Lincoln into the pattern of a mythological demigod had the early start at the printing presses. A series of widely read and often quoted biographies began to appear shortly after Lincoln's death, starting with the Arnold and the Holland lives and running without interruption through the work of Nicolay and Hay and that of Ida M. Tarbell. All were characterized by a highly laudatory tone and all presented Lincoln in an aura of great respectability.

Those who thought of Lincoln as the archetype of the frontiersman were outraged. Herndon was especially bitter at the "Finical fools," the "nice sweet smelling gentlemen" who tried to "handle things with silken gloves & 'a cammel [sic] hair pencil,'" but for personal reasons his own book about Lincoln was delayed for many years. The publication in 1872 of Ward Hill Lamon's biography, ghost-written from Herndonian sources, marked the first widespread circulation in print of the Western version of Lincoln's career. It was greeted as "a national misfortune." When *Herndon's Lincoln* appeared seventeen years later, it, too, met with shrill disapproval, and some shocked souls appealed to Anthony Comstock to suppress this indecent book. This food was too coarse for sensitive stomachs.

It is a mistake to consider these two opposing currents of Lincoln tradition as representing respectively the "ideal" and the "real" Lincoln. Each was legendary in character. The conflict in Lincoln biography between the Holland-Hay-Tarbell faction and the Herndon-Lamon-Weik contingent was not essentially a battle over factual differences; it was more like a religious war. One school portrayed a mythological patron saint; the other, an equally mythological frontier hero. Not all the Lincoln stories related by either school were false, but the facts were at most a secondary consideration. Acceptance or rejection of any Lincoln anecdote depended upon what was fundamentally a religious conviction. Even today this attitude is sometimes found. A recent writer has attacked certain legends that he asserts "libel" Lincoln on two grounds—first, because they "do not create a truer or finer image of him" and, second, because the myths are "unsupported by trustworthy evidence." The order of the reasons deserves notice.

It is widely recognized that the biographies of the Holland school are remote from reality. They present a conventional hero who is discussed from a "frankly eulogistic point of view." The temptation has naturally been to treat their opponents—such as Herndon, Lamon, and Weik—as realists, intent on giving a "true" picture of Lincoln. If there is any meaning left in the word "realism," which is rapidly becoming semantically obsolete, *Herndon's Lincoln* (a biography typical of this latter school) is realistic neither in literary style nor in biographical approach. Herndon's book was dedicated to proving a thesis—that Lincoln had his origin in a "stagnant, putrid pool" and rose through adversity to "the topmost round of the ladder." All of its contents Herndon deliberately arranged to support this contention and to enlist readers' sympathies in behalf of his protagonist. Rough and coarse elements were introduced into the biography, not primarily from conviction that these were vital aspects of human existence, but principally to serve the same function as the villain in the contemporary melodrama. Unlike the true realists, Herndon was concerned with the unusual and the sensational. It is difficult to see how anyone can find in Herndon's emotionalized treatment of the Ann Rutledge legend the work of a biographical or literary realist. Actually, the biographies of the Herndon school are stylized presentations of Western folklore. Herndon's own book recounts the epic of the frontier hero, transmogrified into the pattern of the sentimental novel.

Toward the end of the century the two conceptions of Lincoln—as mythological demigod and as legendary frontier hero—began to blend, sometimes with amusing results. John T. Morse's *Abraham Lincoln*, one of the better early biographies, made no effort to reconcile the two concepts, but accepted both. For Lincoln's early years, Morse followed Herndon, and for the period of the presidency, Nicolay and Hay. The result, he admitted, tended to show that Lincoln was "physically one creature, morally and mentally two beings." In the huge file of newspaper reminiscences in the Lincoln Museum at Fort Wayne one can trace the process by which demigod and hero became inextricably scrambled. By the centennial year of Lincoln's birth the frontier stories that had been considered gamy and rough by an earlier generation had been accepted as typical Lincolnisms; and on the other side, the harshness of the Herndonian outlines was smoothed by the acceptance of many traits from the idealized Lincoln. The result was a "composite American ideal," whose "appeal is stronger than that of other heroes because on him converge so many dear traditions." The current popular conception of Lincoln is "a folk-hero who to the common folk-virtues of shrewdness and kindness adds essential wit and eloquence and loftiness of soul."

V I

ONE MAY QUESTION THE VALUE of studying these legendary accounts of Lincoln. A more conventional procedure is to assault these air castles of contemporary mythology, to use the sharp tools of historical criticism to raze the imaginary structures, to purify the ground by a liberal sprinkling of holy water in the form of footnotes, and to erect a new and "authentic" edifice. Such an approach has its merits. One cannot overestimate the importance of thoroughgoing historical investigation of Lincoln's career; far too little of the huge bibliography of Lincolniana is based upon scholarly, scientific research.

But there is also room for investigation of another sort. Referring to the debunking of historical myths and legends, W. A. Dunning, in his presidential address before the American Historical Association, reminded his hearers that in many cases "influence on the sequence of human affairs has been exercised, not by what really happened, but by what men erroneously believed to have happened." In turning to history for guidance, he observed, men have acted upon "the error that passes as history at the time, not from the truth that becomes known long after." He concluded by pointing out that "for very, very much history there is more importance in the ancient error than in the new-found truth."

His warning applies in the field of Lincoln biography. As J. Frank Dobie has put it, "The history of any public character involves not only the facts about him but what the public has taken to be facts." It is important to examine the Lincoln legends as expressing a collective wish fulfillment of the American people. This is no psychological jargon; it is simply a way of saying that "heroes embody the qualities that we most admire or desire in ourselves." Fully realizing their general inaccuracy and almost universal distortion, the student can use these myths for an understanding of what plain Americans have wished their leaders to be. "If the folk aspiration is worthy, its dreams of great men will be worthy too."

Unless one conceives of time as ending with 1865, the Lincoln of folklore is more significant than the Lincoln of actuality. The historian may prove that the Emancipation actually freed a negligible number of slaves, yet Lincoln continues to live in men's minds as the emancipator of the Negroes. It is this folklore Lincoln who has become the central symbol in American democratic thought; he embodies what ordinary, inarticulate Americans have cherished as ideals. As Ralph H. Gabriel says, he is "first among the folk heroes of the American people." From a study of the Lincoln legends the historian can gain a more balanced insight into the workings of the American mind. As it is now written, intellectual history is too often based on printed sources—sermons, speeches, commencement addresses, books, and newspapers. The result is inevitably a distortion. The men who write books or edit papers are not average citizens. It is much as though the Gallup poll were to interrogate only college presidents. To understand the thinking of ordinary men and women, the historian must delve into their beliefs, their superstitions, their gossip, and their folklore.

The Lincoln ideal offers an excellent starting-point for the investigation. As the pattern has gradually become standardized, the folklore Lincoln is as American as the Mississippi River. Essentially national, the myth is not nationalistic. It reveals the people's faith in the democratic dogma that a poor boy can make good. It demonstrates the incurable romanticism of the American spirit. There is much in the legend that is unpleasant—Lincoln's preternatural cunning, his fondness for Rabelaisian anecdote, his difficulties with his wife—yet these traits seem to be attributed to every real folk hero. The fundamental qualities of the legendary Lincoln emphasize the essential dignity and humanity of our nation's everyday thinking. It speaks well for Americans that to the central hero in their history their folklore has attributed all the decent qualities of civilized man: patience, tolerance, humor, sympathy, kindliness, and sagacity.

THREE

Toward a Reconsideration of Abolitionists

I

ABRAHAM LINCOLN WAS NOT an abolitionist. He believed that slavery was a moral wrong, but he was not sure how to right it. When elected President, he was pledged to contain, not to extirpate, the South's peculiar institution. Only after offers of compensation to slaveholders had failed and after military necessities had become desperate did he issue his Emancipation Proclamation. Even then his action affected only a portion of the Negroes, and the President himself seemed at times unsure of the constitutionality of his proclamation.

It is easy to see, then, why earnest antislavery men were suspicious of Lincoln. Unburdened with the responsibilities of power, unaware of the larger implications of actions, they criticized the President's slowness, doubted his good faith, and hoped for his replacement by a more vigorous emancipationist. Such murmurings and discontents are normal in American political life; in every village over the land there is always at least one man who can tell the President how the government ought to be run.

But a small group of extreme antislavery men, doctrinaire advocates of immediate and uncompensated abolition, assailed the wartime President with a virulence beyond normal expectation. It was one thing to worry about the fixity of Lincoln's principles, but quite another to denounce him, as did Wendell Phillips, as "the slave-hound of Illinois." Many Republicans might reasonably have wanted another candidate in 1864, but there was something almost paranoid in the declaration by a group of Iowa abolitionists that "Lincoln, . . . a Kentuckian by birth, and his brothers-in-law being in the rebel army, is evidently, by his sympathies with the owners of slaves, checked in crushing the rebellion by severe measures against slaveholders." A man might properly be troubled by Lincoln's reconstruction plans, but surely it was excessive for a Parker Pillsbury to pledge that, "by the grace of God and the Saxon Tongue," he would expose the "hypocrisy and cruelty" of Lincoln and of "whatever other President dares tread in his bloody footsteps."

The striking thing here is the disproportion between cause and effect—between Lincoln's actions, which were, after all, against slavery, and the abuse with which abolitionists greeted them. When a patient reacts with excessive vehemence to a mild stimulus, a doctor at once becomes suspicious of some deep-seated malaise. Similarly, the historian should be alert to see in extraordinary and unprovoked violence of expression the symptom of some profound social or psychological dislocation. In this instance, he must ask what produced in these abolitionists their attitude of frozen hostility toward the President.

These abolitionist leaders who so excessively berated Lincoln belonged to a distinct phase of American antislavery agitation. Their demand for an unconditional and immediate end of slavery, which first became articulate around 1830, was different from earlier antislavery sentiment, which had focused on gradual emancipation with colonization of the freed Negroes. And the abolitionist movement, with its Garrisonian deprecation of political action, was also distinct from political antislavery, which became dominant in the 1840's. The abolitionist, then, was a special type of antislavery agitator, and his crusade was part of that remarkable American social phenomenon that erupted in the 1830's, "freedom's ferment," the effervescence of kindred humanitarian reform movements—prohibition; prison reform; education for the blind, deaf, dumb; world peace; penny postage; women's rights; and a score of lesser and more eccentric drives.

Historians have been so absorbed in chronicling what these movements did, in allocating praise or blame among squabbling factions in each, and in making moral judgments on the desirability of various reforms that they have paid surprisingly little attention to the movement as a whole. Few serious attempts have been made to explain why humanitarian reform appeared in America when it did, and more specifically why immediate abolitionism, so different in tone, method, and membership from its predecessors and its successor, emerged in the 1830's.

The participants in such movements naturally give no adequate explanation for such a causal problem. According to their voluminous memoirs and autobiographies, they were simply convinced by religion, by reading, by reflection, that slavery was evil, and they pledged their lives and their sacred honor to destroy it. Seeing slavery in a Southern state, reading an editorial by William Lloyd Garrison, hearing a sermon by Theodore Dwight Weld—such events precipitated a decision made on the highest of moral and ethical planes. No one who has studied the abolitionist literature can doubt the absolute sincerity of these accounts. Abolitionism was a dangerous creed of devotion, and no fair-minded person can believe that men joined the movement for personal gain or for conscious self-glorification. In all truth, the decision to become an antislavery crusader was a decision of conscience.

But when all this is admitted, there are still fundamental problems. Social evils are always present; vice is always in the saddle while virtue trudges on afoot. Not merely the existence of evil but the recognition of it is the prerequisite for reform. Were there more men of integrity, were there more women of sensitive conscience in the 1830's than in any previous decade? A generation of giants these reformers were indeed, but why was there such a concentration of genius in those ten years from 1830 to 1840? If the individual's decision to join the abolitionist movement was a matter of personality or religion or philosophy, is it not necessary to inquire why so many similar personalities or religions or philosophies appeared in America simultaneously? In short, we need to know why so many Americans in the 1830's were predisposed toward a certain kind of reform movement.

Many students have felt, somewhat vaguely, this need for a social interpretation of reform. Little precise analysis has been attempted, but the general histories of antislavery attribute the abolitionist movement to the Christian tradition, to the spirit of the Declaration of Independence, to the ferment of Jacksonian democracy, or to the growth of romanticism. That some or all of these factors may have relation to abolitionism can be granted, but this helps little. Why did the "spirit of Puritanism," to which one writer attributes the movement, become manifest as militant abolitionism in the 1830's although it had no such effect on the previous generation? Why did the Declaration of Independence find fulfillment in abolition during the sixth decade after its promulgation, and not in the fourth or the third?

In their elaborate studies of the antislavery movement,[1] Gilbert H. Barnes and Dwight L. Dumond have pointed up some of the more immediate reasons for the rise of American abolitionism. Many of the most important antislavery leaders fell under the influence of Charles Grandison Finney, whose revivalism set rural New York and the Western Reserve ablaze with religious fervor and evoked "Wonderful outpourings of the Holy Spirit" throughout the North. Not merely did Finney's invocation of the fear of hell and the promise of heaven rouse sluggish souls to renewed religious zeal, but his emphasis upon good works and pious endeavor as steps toward salvation freed men's minds from the bonds of arid theological controversies. One of Finney's most famous converts was Theodore Dwight Weld, the greatest of the Western abolitionists, "eloquent as an angel and powerful as thunder," who recruited a band of seventy antislavery apostles, trained them in Finney's

[1] Gilbert H. Barnes, *The Antislavery Impulse, 1830–1844* (1933); Barnes and Dwight L. Dumond, eds., *Letters of Theodore Dwight Weld, Angelina Grimké Weld and Sarah Grimké, 1822–1844* (2 vols., 1934); Dumond, ed., *Letters of James Gillespie Birney, 1831–1857* (2 vols., 1939); Dumond, *Antislavery Origins of the Civil War in the United States* (1939).

revivalistic techniques, and sent them forth to consolidate the emancipation movement in the North. Their greatest successes were reaped in precisely those communities where Finney's preaching had prepared the soil.

Barnes and Dumond also recognized the importance of British influence upon the American antislavery movement. The connection is clear and easily traced: British antislavery leaders fought for immediate emancipation in the West Indies; reading the tracts of Wilbeforce and Clarkson converted William Lloyd Garrison to immediate abolitionism at about the same time that Theodore Weld was won over to the cause by his English friend Charles Stuart; and Weld in turn gained for the movement the support of the Tappan brothers, the wealthy New York merchants and philanthropists who contributed so much in money and time to the antislavery crusade. Thus, abolition had in British precedent a model, in Garrison and Weld leaders, and in the Tappans financial backers.

Historians are deeply indebted to Professors Barnes and Dumond, for the importance of their studies on the antislavery movement is very great. But perhaps they have raised as many questions as they have answered. Both religious revivalism and British antislavery theories had a selective influence in America. Many men heard Finney and Weld, but only certain communities were converted. Hundreds of Americans read Wilberforce, Clarkson, and the other British abolitionists, but only the Garrisons and the Welds were convinced. The question remains: Whether they received the idea through the revivalism of Finney or through the publication of British antislavery spokesmen, why were some Americans in the 1830's for the first time moved to advocate immediate abolition? Why was this particular seed bed ready at this precise time?

II

I BELIEVE that the best way to answer this difficult question is to analyze the leadership of the abolitionist movement. There is, unfortunately, no complete list of American abolitionists, and I have had to use a good deal of subjective judgment in drawing up a roster of leading reformers. From the classified indexes of the *Dictionary of American Biography* and the old Appleton's *Cyclopaedia of American Biography* and from important primary and secondary works on the reform generation, I made a list of about two hundred and fifty persons who seemed to be identified with the antislavery cause. This obviously is not a definitive enumeration of all the important abolitionists; had someone else compiled it, other names doubtless would have been included. Nevertheless, even if one or two major spokesmen have accidentally been omitted, this is a good deal more than a representative sampling of antislavery leadership.

After preliminary work I eliminated nearly one hundred of these names. Some proved not to be genuine abolitionists but advocates of colonizing the freed Negroes in Africa; others had only incidental interest or sympathy for emancipation. I ruthlessly excluded those who joined the abolitionists after 1840, because the political antislavery movement clearly poses a different set of causal problems. After this weeding out, I had reluctantly to drop other names because I was unable to secure more than random bits of information about them. Some of Weld's band of seventy agitators, for instance, were so obscure that even Barnes and Dumond were unable to identify them. There remained the names of one hundred and six abolitionists, the hard core of active antislavery leadership in the 1830's.

Most of these abolitionists were born between 1790 and 1810, and when the first number of the *Liberator* was published in 1831, their median age was twenty-nine. Abolitionism was thus a revolt of the young.

My analysis confirms the traditional identification of radical antislavery with New England. Although I made every effort to include Southern and Western leaders, eighty-five per cent of these abolitionists came from Northeastern states, sixty per cent from New England, thirty per cent from Massachusetts alone. Many of the others were descended from New England families. Only four of the leaders were born abroad or were second-generation immigrants.

The ancestors of these abolitionists are in some ways as interesting as the antislavery leaders themselves. In the biographies of their more famous descendants certain standard phrases recur: "of the best New England stock," "of Pilgrim descent," "of a serious, pious household." The parents of the leaders generally belonged to a clearly defined stratum of society. Many were preachers, doctors, or teachers; some were farmers and a few were merchants; but only three were manufacturers (and two of these on a very small scale), none was a banker, and only one was an ordinary day laborer. Virtually all the parents were stanch Federalists.

These families were neither rich nor poor, and it is worth remembering that among neither extreme did abolitionism flourish. The abolitionist could best appeal to "the substantial men" of the community, thought Weld, and not to "the *aristocracy* and fashionable worldliness" that remained aloof from reform. In *The Burned-Over District*, an important analysis of reform drives in western New York, Whitney R. Cross has confirmed Weld's social analysis. In New York, antislavery was strongest in those counties which had once been economically dominant but which by the 1830's, though still prosperous, had relatively fallen behind their more advantageously situated neighbors. As young men the fathers of abolitionists had been leaders of their communities and states; in their old age they were elbowed aside by the merchant prince, the manufacturing tycoon, the corporation lawyer. The bustling democracy of the 1830's passed them by; as the Reverend Ludovicus Weld lamented to his famous son Theodore: "I have . . . felt like a stranger in a strange land."

If the abolitionists were descendants of old and distinguished New England families, it is scarcely surprising to find among them an enthusiasm for higher education. The women in the movement could not, of course, have much formal education, nor could the three Negroes here included, but of the eighty-nine white male leaders, at least fifty-three attended college, university, or theological seminary. In the East, Harvard and Yale were the favored schools; in the West, Oberlin; but in any case the training was usually of the traditional liberal arts variety.

For an age of chivalry and repression there was an extraordinary proportion of women in the abolitionist movement. Fourteen of these leaders were women who defied the convention that the female's place was at the fireside, not in the forum, and appeared publicly as antislavery apostles. The Grimké sisters of South Carolina were the most famous of these, but most of the antislavery heroines came from New England.

It is difficult to tabulate the religious affiliations of antislavery leaders. Most were troubled by spiritual discontent, and they wandered from one sect to another seeking salvation. It is quite clear, however, that there was a heavy Congregational-Presbyterian and Quaker preponderance. There were many Methodists, some Baptists, but very few Unitarians, Episcopalians, or Catholics. Admirable dissertations on the antislavery movement in each of the Western states, prepared at the University of Michigan under Professor Dumond's supervision, confirm the conclusion that, except in Pennsylvania, it is correct to consider humanitarian reform and Congregational-Presbyterianism as causally interrelated.

Only one of these abolitionist leaders seems to have had much connection with the rising industrialism of the 1830's, and only thirteen of the entire group were born in any of the principal cities of the United States. Abolition was distinctly a rural movement, and throughout the crusade many of the antislavery leaders seemed to feel an instinctive antipathy toward the city. Weld urged his following: "Let the great cities *alone*; they must be burned down by *back fires*. The springs to touch in order to move them *lie in the country*."

In general the abolitionists had little sympathy or understanding for the problems of an urban society. Reformers though they were, they were men of conservative economic views. Living in an age of growing industrialization, of tenement congestion, of sweatshop oppression, not one of them can properly be identified with the labor movement of the 1830's. Most would agree with Garrison, who denounced labor leaders for trying "to inflame the minds of our working classes against the more opulent, and to persuade men that they are contemned and oppressed by a wealthy aristocracy." After all, Wendell Phillips assured the laborers, the American factory operative could be "neither wronged nor oppressed" so long as he had the ballot. William Ellery Channing, gentle high priest of the Boston area, told dissatisfied miners that moral self-improvement was a more potent weapon than strikes, and he urged that they take advantage of the leisure afforded by unemployment for mental and spiritual self-cultivation. A Massachusetts attempt to limit the hours of factory operatives to ten a day was denounced by Samuel Gridley Howe, veteran of a score of humanitarian wars, as "emasculating the people" because it took from them their free right to choose their conditions of employment.

The suffering of laborers during periodic depressions aroused little sympathy among abolitionists. As Emerson remarked tartly, "Do not tell me . . . of my obligation to put all poor men in good situations. Are they *my* poor? I tell thee, thou foolish philanthropist, that I grudge the dollar, the dime, the cent I give to such men. . . ."

Actually it is clear that abolitionists were not so much hostile to labor as indifferent to it. The factory worker represented an alien and unfamiliar system toward which the antislavery leaders felt no kinship or responsibility. Sons of the old New England of Federalism, farming, and foreign commerce, the reformers did not fit into a society that was beginning to be dominated by a bourgeoisie based on manufacturing and trade. Thoreau's bitter comment, "We do not ride on the railroads; they ride on us," was more than the acid aside of a man whose privacy at Walden had been invaded; it was the reaction of a class whose leadership had been discarded. The bitterest attacks in the journals of Ralph Waldo Emerson, the most pointed denunciations in the sermons of Theodore Parker, the harshest philippics in the orations of Charles Sumner were directed against the "Lords of the Loom," not so much for exploiting their labor as for changing the character and undermining the morality of old New England.

As Lewis Tappan pointed out in a pamphlet suggestively titled *Is It Right to Be Rich?*, reformers did not object to ordinary acquisition of money. It was instead that "eagerness to amass property" which made a man "selfish, unsocial, mean, tyrannical, and but a nominal Christian" that seemed so wrong. It is worth noting that Tappan, in his numerous examples of the vice of excessive accumulation, found this evil stemming from manufacturing and banking, and never from farming or foreign trade—in which last occupation Tappan himself flourished.

Tappan, like Emerson, was trying to uphold the old standards and to protest against the easy morality of the new age. "This invasion of Nature by Trade with its Money, its Credit, its Steam, its Railroads," complained Emerson, "threatens to upset the balance of man, and establish a new universal monarchy more tyrannical than Babylon or Rome." Calmly Emerson welcomed the panic of 1837 as a wholesome lesson to the new monarchs of manufacturing: "I see good in such emphatic and universal calamity. . . ."

Jacksonian democracy, whether considered a labor movement or a triumph of laissez-faire capitalism, obviously had little appeal for the abolitionist conservative. As far as can be determined, only one of these abolitionist leaders was a Jacksonian; nearly all were strong Whigs. William Lloyd Garrison made his first public appearance in Boston to endorse the arch-Whig Harrison Gray Otis; James G. Birney campaigned throughout Alabama to defeat Jackson; Henry B. Stanton wrote editorials for anti-Jackson newspapers. Not merely the leaders but their followers as well seem to have been hostile to Jacksonian democracy, for it is estimated that fifty-nine out of sixty Massachusetts abolitionists belonged to the Whig party.

Jacksonian Democrats recognized the opposition of the abolitionists and accused the leaders of using slavery to distract public attention from more immediate economic problems at home. "The abolitionists of the North have mistaken the color of the American slaves," Theophilus Fisk wrote tartly; "all the real Slaves in the United States have pale faces. . . . I will venture to affirm that there are more slaves in Lowell and Nashua alone than can be found South of the Potomac."

III

HERE, THEN, is a composite portrait of abolitionist leadership. Descended from old and socially dominant Northeastern families, reared in a faith of aggressive piety and moral endeavor, educated for conservative leadership, these young men and women who reached maturity in the 1830's faced a strange and hostile world. Social and economic leadership was being transferred from the country to the city, from the farmer to the manufacturer, from the preacher to the corporation attorney. Too distinguished a family, too gentle an education, too nice a morality were handicaps in a bustling world of business. Expecting to lead, these young people found no followers. They were an elite without function, a displaced class in American society.

Some—like Daniel Webster—made their terms with the new order and lent their talents and their family names to the greater glorification of the god of trade. But many of the young men were unable to overcome their traditional disdain for the new money-grubbing class that was beginning to rule. In these plebeian days they could not be successful in politics; family tradition and education prohibited idleness; and agitation allowed the only chance for personal and social self-fulfillment.

If the young men were aliens in the new industrial society, the young women felt equally lost. Their mothers had married preachers, doctors, teachers, and had become dominant moral forces in their communities. But in rural New England of the 1830's the westward exodus had thinned the ranks of eligible suitors, and because girls of distinguished family hesitated to work in the cotton mills, more and more turned to schoolteaching and nursing and other socially useful but unrewarding spinster tasks. The women, like the men, were ripe for reform.

They did not support radical economic reforms because fundamentally these young men and women had no serious quarrel with the capitalistic system of private ownership and control of property. What they did question, and what they did rue, was the transfer of leadership to the wrong groups in society, and their appeal for reform was a strident call for their own class to re-exert its former social dominance. Some fought for prison reform; some for women's rights; some for world peace; but ultimately most came to make that natural identification between moneyed aristocracy, textile manufacturing, and Southern slave-grown cotton. An attack on slavery was their best, if quite unconscious, attack upon the new industrial system. As Richard Henry Dana, Jr., avowed: "I am a Free Soiler, because I am . . . of the stock of the old Northern gentry, and have a particular dislike to any subserviency on the part of our people to the slave-holding oligarchy"—and, he might have added, to their Northern manufacturing allies.

With all its dangers and all its sacrifices, membership in a movement like abolitionism offered these young people a chance for a reassertion of their traditional values, an opportunity for association with others of their kind, and a possibility of achieving that self-fulfillment which should traditionally have been theirs as social leaders. Reform gave meaning to the lives of this displaced social elite. "My life, what has it been?" queried one young seeker; "the panting of a soul after eternity—the feeling that there was nothing here to fill the aching void, to provide enjoyment and occupation such as my spirit panted for. The world, what has it been? a howling wilderness. I seem to be just now awakened . . . to a true perception of the end of my being, my duties, my responsibilities, the rich and perpetual pleasures which God has provided for us in the fulfillment of duty to Him and to our fellow creatures. Thanks to the A[nti]. S[lavery]. cause, it first gave an impetus to my palsied intellect. . . ."

Viewed against the backgrounds and common ideas of its leaders, abolitionism appears to have been a double crusade. Seeking freedom for the Negro in the South, these reformers were also attempting a restoration of the traditional values of their class at home. Leadership of humanitarian reform may have been influenced by revivalism or by British precedent, but its true origin lay in the drastic dislocation of Northern society. Basically, abolitionism should be considered the anguished protest of an aggrieved class against a world they never made.

Such an interpretation helps explain the abolitionists' excessive suspicion of Abraham Lincoln. Not merely did the President, with his plebeian origins, his lack of Calvinistic zeal, his success in corporate law practice, and his skill in practical politics, personify the very forces that they thought most threatening in Northern society, but by his effective actions against slavery he left the abolitionists without a cause. The freeing of the slaves ended the great crusade that had brought purpose and joy to the abolitionists. For them Abraham Lincoln was not the Great Emancipator; he was the killer of the dream.

FOUR

An Excess of Democracy: The American Civil War and the Social Process

ABOUT FEW SUBJECTS do historians become so excited as about the causes of wars. War is by its nature such a monstrous evil that rational man seeks desperately to "explain" it. Most Western historians, mild men with humane intentions, can but instinctively regard war as a hideous aberration, a foul blot in the human copybook.

American historians have been especially concerned with this problem. Nearly all nurtured in a comfortable belief in progress, they have found it necessary to face the fact that the United States has not always marched onward and upward but has repeatedly backslid into the abyss of savagery. For most American wars our historians have a comforting explanation: they were caused by somebody else. It was the British, we say, who provoked the American Revolution and the War of 1812; it was the Mexicans who incited the War of 1846; it was Spanish barbarities in Cuba that produced the War of 1898; it was German submarine atrocities that caused American entrance into World War I; it was the Japanese attack at Pearl Harbor that brought us into World War II; it was Communist aggression in Korea that sent American soldiers to fight in that God-forsaken land.

But the most sanguinary of American conflicts does not lend itself to such an explanation. The American Civil War of 1861–65 can be blamed upon nobody but the American participants themselves. It is partly for this reason that the causes of our Civil War have had an irresistible fascination for Americans. Virtually every imaginative writer of any importance in the United States since the 1860's has felt obliged to deal with this brothers' war and the subsequent reconciliation. Novelists as diverse as Mark Twain and Henry James, Stephen Crane and Thomas Nelson Page, Margaret Mitchell and William Faulkner have exhibited a recurring, almost obsessive interest in this wholly American war. Almost every major historian of the United States has also been concerned with the problem; one thinks, for example, of Henry Adams, Edward Channing, James Ford Rhodes, John Bach McMaster, James Schouler, Hermann E. von Holst, Albert J. Beveridge, and James G. Randall.

Though united in concern to explain the appalling catastrophe that befell America in the 1860's, historians of the United States have agreed upon very little else about that conflict. Many have continued to support James Ford Rhodes's flat contention that the American Civil War had "a single cause, slavery"; others have accepted Allan Nevins's modification that the cause was not Negro slavery alone but the concomitant problem of race adjustment. Disciples of Frederick Jackson Turner have found the cause of the Civil War in the growth of sectionalism, especially in the competition between sections for the newly opened West. Followers of Charles A. Beard, on the other hand, have traced the essential origin of the war to the clash of economic classes, chiefly to the inevitable conflict between Northern capitalism and Southern agrarianism. The "Revisionists" of the 1930's and 1940's, headed by Avery O. Craven and James G. Randall, argued that the Civil War had no basic causes; that it was a "repressible conflict," a "needless war," precipitated through want of wisdom in the "blundering generation" of the 1850's. More recently, critics, who styled themselves "New Nationalists," have replied sharply that the Revisionists were blind to the enormous evil of slavery and sought "in optimistic sentimentalism an escape from the severe demands of moral decision."

Acrimoniously, American historians have argued over the degree to which individual politicians and statesmen were responsible for the Civil War. Presidents Franklin Pierce, James Buchanan, and Abraham Lincoln have all been accused of bringing on the war, but all three have had vigorous defenders. George Fort Milton and other scholars rehabilitated the reputation of Stephen A. Douglas as the statesman of sectional conciliation, but Allan Nevins continued to brand the Illinois "Little Giant" as a morally obtuse and disastrously short-sighted politician. Frank L. Owsley, a Southern-born historian, squarely blamed Northern abolitionists; "neither Dr. Goebbels nor Virginio Gayda nor Stalin's propaganda agents," he wrote in 1941, "were able to plumb the depths of vulgarity and obscenity reached and maintained by . . . Wendell Phillips, Charles Sumner, and other abolitionists of note." Historians of Northern origin retorted angrily that the blame should more properly fall upon Southern "fire-eaters," who precipitated secession. Craven and Randall attacked with equal vigor the "extremists" and "agitators" of all sections, the disciples of John C. Calhoun along with the followers of William Lloyd Garrison.

It is sometimes mistakenly thought that the basic issue over which these historians have so confusingly argued is that of the inevitability of the Civil War. Such a view is an oversimplification, for, as the Dutch historian Pieter Geyl sensibly remarks, "The question of evitability or inevitability is one on which the historian can never form any but an ambivalent opinion." So much depends upon speculations that historians are properly reluctant to make. If Jefferson Davis's government had refused to fight for independence, there could, of course, have been no war. Similarly, if Lincoln's administration had acquiesced in the peaceful secession of the South, there would have been no conflict. The question of inevitability is also partly a matter of timing. Virtually no one would argue that a Civil War was inescapable as early as 1820 or 1830; hardly anyone would suggest that it was avoidable after the first gun was fired on Fort Sumter.

The real cleavage in American historical thought is, instead, between those who see the Civil War as the result of the operation of grand elemental forces and those who attribute it to the working of accidental or random factors. The former discuss the war as the result of deep national urges, basic social or economic cleavages, and fundamental nationalistic drives; the latter argue that these alleged fundamental "causes" have no demonstrated connection with the course of events in the 1850's and stress the importance of accident, of personality, and of propaganda in shaping history.

Neither of these rival interpretations is entirely satisfactory. The "Fundamentalists" (if we may so call them) have failed to prove that their underlying "causes" produced the actual outbreak of hostilities. They talk impressively about Southern economic grievances—but never demonstrate that such issues as the tariff or internal improvements played any significant part in bringing on the actual secession crisis. The rise of Southern nationalism is another of these general explanations that sound impressive—until one realizes, after making a study of the Confederacy, that Southern nationalism during the Civil War was anything but a strong unifying force. It is plausible to stress slavery as the cause of the Civil War, but, as Revisionists repeatedly pointed out, no responsible political body in the North in 1860 proposed to do anything at all about slavery where it actually existed and no numerous group of Southerners thought their peculiar institution could be extended into the free states. As for Allan Nevins's emphasis upon the problems of race adjustment, one must note that virtually nobody, North or South, was concerned with such matters in the 1850's.

The problem with all these Fundamentalist explanations is that they rely upon stereotypes that have little relation to the complex social reality of the United States in the 1850's. Writers speak of the Southern interest in slavery, even when they perfectly well know that in the "plantation" South only one fourth of the white families owned any slaves at all. They talk of "industrial" New England, though over half of the population of that region still lived on farms. They write of the small farmers of the "frontier" West, even though that section had a remarkable urban development and even though it was partly settled by men like Michael Sullivant, "the world's largest farmer," who owned 80,000 acres of rich Illinois soil, employed between 100 and 200 laborers, and had 5,000 head of cattle grazing in his own pastures.

On the other hand, it is equally difficult to accept the Revisionist argument that apparently random developments—such as the introduction of the Kansas-Nebraska Bill in 1854 or John Brown's raid—produced the war, if only because one dislikes to give up the old maxim that great events have great causes. If it is true that the hottest issue of the 1850's was not race adjustment or the future of slavery itself but the spread of slavery into the few remaining territories of the United States, do we not have to inquire why public opinion, North and South, grew so sensitive over what appears to be an abstract and unimportant point? If we must admit that propagandists and agitators, abolitionists and fire-eaters, whipped up sentiment in both sections, are we not required to ask further why that public opinion could be thus aroused, and why on these specific issues? And if we are bound to agree that the 1850's saw a failure of American statesmanship, do we not have to seek why this disaster afflicted the United States at this particular time and in this peculiar manner?

I

SINCE NEITHER REVISIONISM nor Fundamentalism offers an intellectually satisfying explanation for the coming of the Civil War, perhaps the problem should be approached afresh. The Civil War, I believe, can best be understood neither as the result of accident nor as the product of conflicting sectional interests, but as the outgrowth of social processes that affected the entire United States during the first half of the nineteenth century.

It is remarkable how few historians have attempted to deal with American society as a whole during this critical period. Accustomed to looking upon it as a prewar era, we have stressed divisive elements and factors of sectional conflict. Contemporary European observers, on the whole, had a better perspective. Some of these foreign travelers looked upon the American experiment with loathing; others longed for its success; but nearly all stressed the basic unity of American culture, minimizing the 10 percent of ideas and traits that were distinctive to the individual sections and stressing the 90 percent of attitudes and institutions that all Americans shared.

It is time for us to emulate the best of these European observers and to draw a broad picture of the common American values in the early nineteenth century. Any such analysis would have to start with the newness of American life. Novelty was the keynote not merely for the recently settled regions of the West but for all of American society. Though states like Virginia and Massachusetts had two hundred years of history behind them, they, too, were affected by social changes so rapid as to require each generation to start anew. In the Northeast the rise of the city shockingly disrupted the normal course of societal evolution. Boston, for example, grew from a tidy, inbred city of 40,000 in 1830 to a sprawling, unmanageable metropolis of 178,000 by 1860; New York leaped from 515,000 to 805,000 in the single decade of the 1850's. This kind of urban life was as genuinely a frontier experience as settling on the Great Plains; to hundreds of thousands of European-born immigrants and American farm boys and girls, moving to the big city was an enormously exhilarating and unsettling form of pioneering. In the Old South the long-settled states of the Eastern coast were undergoing a parallel evolution, for the opening of rich alluvial lands along the Gulf Coast offered bonanzas as surely as did the gold mines of California. In the early nineteenth century all sections of the United States were being transformed with such rapidity that stability and security were everywhere vanishing values; nowhere could a father safely predict what kind of world his son would grow up in.

Plenty was another characteristic of this new American society. From the richness of the country's basic resources, Americans, as David M. Potter observed, ought to be called "The People of Plenty." The lands begged to be developed. Immigrants from less privileged lands found it almost impossible to credit the abundance that everywhere surrounded them. As settlers in the Wabash Valley sang:

> *Way down upon the Wabash*
> *Such lands were never known.*
> *If Adam had passed over it,*

This soil he'd surely own.
He'd think it was the Garden
He played in when a boy,
And straight he'd call it Eden
In the State of Illinois.

Mineral wealth surpassed men's dreams. And there was nothing to divert Americans from the exploitation of their resources. As Tocqueville pointed out, the absence of strong neighbors to the north and the south gave the United States a peculiar position among the nineteenth-century powers; she alone could devote her entire energies to the creation of wealth, instead of wasting them upon arms and warlike preparations. Some Americans made their fortunes in manufacturing; others in cotton and rice plantations; still others in the mines and lands of the West. Not everybody got rich, of course, but everybody aspired to do so. Both the successful and those less fortunate were equally ruthless in exploiting the country's natural resources, whether of water power, of fertile fields, of mineral wealth, or simply of human labor.

Rapid social mobility was another dominant American trait. Though some recent sociological studies have correctly warned us that the Horatio Alger stories represent a myth rather than a reality of American society and that, even in the early nineteenth century, education, family standing, and inherited wealth were valuable assets, we must not forget that there was nevertheless an extraordinary opportunity in the United States for poor boys to make good. Surely in no other Western society of the period could a self-taught merchant's apprentice have founded the manufacturing dynasty of the Massachusetts Lawrences; or a semiliterate ferryboatman named Vanderbilt have gained control of New York City's transportation system; or the son of a London dried-fish shopkeeper named Benjamin have become Senator from Louisiana; or a self-taught prairie lawyer have been elected President of the nation.

Such vertical mobility was not confined to any class or section in the United States. Though most of us are willing to accept the rags-to-riches version of frontier society, we often fail to realize that everywhere in America the early nineteenth century was the day of the self-made man. The Boston Brahmins, as Cleveland Amory wittily pointed out, were essentially *nouveaux riches*; the Proper Bostonians' handsome houses on Beacon Hill, their affectations of social superiority, their illusions of hearing ancestral voices concealed the fact that most of them derived from quite humble origins, and within the last generation or two. In the South there were, of course, a few fine old families—but not nearly so many as the F.F.V.'s fondly fancied—but these were not the leaders of Southern society. The typical figure of the antebellum South is not Robert E. Lee but tight-fisted Thomas Sutpen, William Faulkner's fictional character, whose unscrupulous rise from hardscrabble beginnings to the planter class is traced in *Absalom, Absalom.*

II

A NEW SOCIETY OF PLENTY, with abundant opportunities for self-advancement, was bound to leave its hallmark upon its citizens, whether they lived in North, South, or West. The connection between character and culture is still an essentially unexplored one, but it is surely no accident that certain widely shared characteristics appeared among Americans in every rank of life. In such a society, richly endowed with every natural resource, protected against serious foreign wars, and structured so as to encourage men to rise, it was inevitable that a faith in progress should be generally shared. The idea of progress is not, of course, an American invention, and no claim is even suggested here that nineteenth-century Americans were unique. Indeed, the American experience is merely a special case of the sweeping social transformation that was more slowly changing Europe as well. But American circumstances did make for a particularly verdant belief that betterment, whether economic, social, or moral, was just around the corner. Surely Mark Twain's Colonel Beriah Sellers is, if not a unique American type, the representative American citizen of his age.

Confidence in the future encouraged Americans in their tendency to speculate. A man of even very modest means might anticipate making his fortune, not through exertions of his own, but through the waves of prosperity that seemed constantly to float American values higher and higher. A small initial capital could make a man another John Jacob Astor. "I have now a young man in my mind," wrote C. C. Andrews from Minnesota in 1856, "who came to a town ten miles this side of St. Paul, six months ago, with $400. He commenced trading, and has already, by good investments and the profits of his business, doubled his money." It was no wonder that Americans rejected the safe investment, the "sure thing," to try a flier into the unknown. In some cases the American speculative mania was pathological. A writer in November 1849 described the frenzied state of mind of Californians:

> The people of San Francisco are mad, stark mad. . . . A
> dozen times or more, during the last few weeks, I have
> been taken by the arm by some of the *millionaires*—so
> they call themselves, I call them madmen—of San Fran-
> cisco, looking wondrously dirty and out at elbows for men
> of such magnificent pretensions. They have dragged me
> about, through the mud and filth almost up to my middle,
> from one pine box to another, called mansion, hotel,
> bank, or store, as it may please the imagination, and have
> told me, with a sincerity that would have done credit to the
> Bedlamite, that these splendid . . . structures were theirs,
> and they, the fortunate proprietors, were worth from two to
> three hundred thousand dollars a year each.

But one does not have to turn to the gold rush of California to learn what abundance can do to social values. A sympathetic contemporary Southerner, Joseph G. Baldwin, described "The Flush Times in Mississippi and Alabama," when the virgin lands in that region were first opened to settlement:

... the new era had set in—the era of the second great experiment of independence: the experiment, namely, of credit without capital, and enterprise without honesty. . . . Every cross-road and every avocation presented an opening—through which a fortune was seen by the adventurer in near perspective. Credit was a thing of course. To refuse it—if the thing was ever done—were an insult for which a bowie-knife were not a too summary or exemplary means of redress . . . prices rose like smoke. Lots in obscure villages were held at city prices; lands, bought at the minimum cost of government, were sold at from thirty to forty dollars an acre. . . . Society was wholly unorganized: there was no restraining public opinion: the law was well-nigh powerless—and religion scarcely was heard of except as furnishing the oaths and *technics* of profanity. . . . Money, got without work, . . . turned the heads of its possessors, and they spent it with a recklessness like that with which they gained it. The pursuits of industry neglected, riot and coarse debauchery filled up the vacant hours. . . . The . . . doggeries [i.e., saloons] . . . were in full blast in those days, no village having less than a half-dozen all busy all the time: gaming and horseracing were polite and well patronized amusements. . . . Occasionally the scene was diversified by a murder or two, which though perpetrated from behind a corner, or behind the back of the deceased, whenever the accused *chose* to stand his trial, was always found to have been committed in self-defense. . . . The old rules of business and the calculations of prudence were alike disregarded, and profligacy, in all the departments . . . , held riotous carnival. Larceny grew not only respectable, but genteel, and ruffled it in all the pomp of purple and fine linen. Swindling was raised to the dignity of the fine arts. Felony came forth from its covert, put on more seemly habiliments, and took its seat with unabashed front in the upper places of the synagogue. . . .

> "Commerce was king"—and Rag, Tag and Bobtail his cabinet council. . . . The condition of society may be imagined:—vulgarity—ignorance—fussy and arrogant pretension—unmitigated rowdyism—bullying insolence. . . .

Allowance must of course be made for a writer of imaginative fiction, but there is a basic truth in Baldwin's observations. In nineteenth-century America all the recognized values of orderly civilization were gradually being eroded. Social atomization affected every segment of American society. All too accurately Tocqueville portrayed the character of the new generation of Southerners: "The citizen of the Southern states becomes a sort of domestic dictator from infancy; the first notion he acquires in life is that he was born to command, and the first habit he contracts is that of ruling without resistance. His education tends, then, to give him the character of a haughty and hasty man—irascible, violent, ardent in his desires, impatient of obstacles." William H. Herndon, Lincoln's law partner, graphically depicted the even cruder settlers in the West:

> These men could shave a horse's main [sic] and tail, paint, disfigure and offer him for sale to the owner in the very act of inquiring for his own horse. . . . They could hoop up in a hogshead a drunken man, they being themselves drunk, put in and nail down the head, and roll the man down New Salem hill a hundred feet or more. They could run down a lean, hungry wild pig, catch it, heat a ten-plate stove furnace hot, and putting in the pig, could cook it, they dancing the while a merry jig.

Even the most intimate domestic relations were drastically altered in nineteenth-century America. For centuries the Western tradition had been one in which females were subordinate to males, and in which the wife found her full being only in her husband. But in the pre–Civil War United States such a social order was no longer possible. In Massachusetts, for example, which in 1850 had 17,480 more females than males, many women could no longer look for fulfilment in marriage and a family; if they were from the lower classes they must labor to support themselves, and if they were from the upper classes they must find satisfaction in charitable deeds and humanitarian enterprises. It is not altogether surprising that so many reform movements had their roots in New England. In the West, on the other hand, women were at a great premium; however old or ugly, they found themselves marriageable. One reads, for example, of a company of forty-one women who traveled from the East to frontier Iowa. Before their steamship could reach the wharf, the shore was crowded with men using megaphones to make proposals of marriage. "Miss with the blue ribbon in your bonnet, will you take me?" "Hallo thar, gal, with a cinnamon shawl; if agreeable we will jine." It was, consequently, extremely difficult to persuade these ladies that, after marriage, they had no legal existence except as chattels of their husbands. Not surprisingly, woman's suffrage, as a practical movement, flourished in the West.

Children in such a society of abundance were an economic asset. A standard toast to wedding couples was: "Health to the groom, and here's to the bride, thumping luck, and big children." Partly because they were so valuable, children were well cared for and given great freedom. Virtually every European traveler in the nineteenth century remarked the uncurbed egotism of the American child: "Boys assume the air of full grown coxcombs." "Parents have no command over their children." "The children's faces were dirty, their hair uncombed, their disposition evidently untaught, and all the members of the family, from the boy of six years of age up to the owner (I was going to say master) of the house, appeared independent of each other." "The lad of fourteen . . . struts and swaggers and smokes his cigar and drinks rum; treads on the toes of his grandfather, swears at his mother and sister, and vows that he will run away . . . the children govern the parents."

This child was father of the American man. It is no wonder that Tocqueville, attempting to characterize nineteenth-century American society, was obliged to invent a new word, "individualism." This is not to argue that there were in pre–Civil War America no men of orderly, prudent, and conservative habits; it is to suggest that rarely in human history has a people as a whole felt itself so completely unfettered by precedent. In a nation so new that, as President James K. Polk observed, its history was in the future, in a land of such abundance, men felt under no obligation to respect the lessons of the past. Even in the field of artistic and literary endeavor acceptance of classical forms or acquiescence in the dictates of criticism was regarded as evidence of inferiority. Ralph Waldo Emerson set the theme for nineteenth-century Americans: "Let me admonish you, first of all, to go alone; to refuse the good models, even those which are sacred in the imagination of men . . . Imitation cannot go above its model. The imitator dooms himself to hopeless mediocrity. . . . Yourself a newborn bard of the Holy Ghost, cast behind you all conformity. . . ."

Every aspect of American life witnessed this desire to throw off precedent and to rebel from authority. Every institution that laid claim to prescriptive right was challenged and overthrown. The Church, that potent instrument of social cohesion in the colonial period, was first disestablished, and then strange new sects, such as the Shakers, Mormons, and Campbellites, appeared to fragment the Christian community. The squirearchy, once a powerful conservative influence in the Middle States and the South, was undermined by the abolition of primogeniture and entails and then was directly defied in the Anti-Rent War of New York. All centralizing economic institutions came under attack. The Second Bank of the United States, which exercised a healthy restraint upon financial chaos, was destroyed during the Jackson period, and at the same time the Supreme Court moved to strike down vested monopoly rights.

Nowhere was the American rejection of authority more complete than in the political sphere. The decline in the powers of the Federal government from the constructive centralism of George Washington's administration to the feeble vacillation of James Buchanan's is so familiar as to require no repetition here. With declining powers there went also declining respect. Leonard D. White's scholarly works on American administrative history accurately trace the descending status and the decreasing skill of the Federal government employees. The national government, moreover, was not being weakened in order to bolster the state governments, for they too were decreasing in power. The learned historians of Massachusetts during these years, Oscar and Mary Handlin, found the theme of their story in the abandonment of the idea of "Commonwealth," in the gradual forgetting of the ideal of the purposeful state that had once concerted the interests of all its subordinate groups. By the 1850's the authority of all government in America was at a low point; government to the American was, at most, merely an institution with a negative role, a guardian of fair play.

Declining power of government was paralleled by increased popular participation in it. The extension of the suffrage in America has rarely been the result of a concerted reform drive, such as culminated in England in 1832 and in 1867; rather it has been part of the gradual erosion of all authority, of the feeling that restraints and differentials are necessarily antidemocratic, and of the practical fact that such restrictions are difficult to enforce. By the mid–nineteenth century in most American states white manhood suffrage was virtually universal.

All too rarely have historians given sufficient attention to the consequences of the extension of the franchise in America, an extension that was only one aspect of the general democratic rejection of authority. Different appeals must necessarily be made to a broad electorate than to an *élite* group. Since the rival parties must both woo the mass of voters, both tended to play down issues and to stand on broad equivocal platforms that evaded all subjects of controversy. Candidates were selected not because of their demonstrated statesmanship but because of their high public visibility. The rash of military men who ran for President in the 1840's and 1850's was no accident. If it is a bit too harsh to say that extension of the suffrage inevitably produced leaders without policies and parties without principles, it can be safely maintained that universal democracy made it difficult to deal with issues requiring subtle understanding and delicate handling. Walter Bagehot, that shrewd English observer, was one of the few commentators who accurately appreciated the changes that universal suffrage brought to American life. Writing in October 1861, he declared:

The steadily augmenting power of the lower orders in America has naturally augmented the dangers of the Federal Union . . . a dead level of universal suffrage runs, more or less, over the whole length of the United States . . . it places the entire control over the political action of the whole State in the hands of common labourers, who are of all classes the least instructed—of all the most aggressive—of all the most likely to be influenced by local animosity—of all the most likely to exaggerate every momentary sentiment—of all the least likely to be capable of a considerable toleration for the constant oppositions of opinion, the not infrequent differences of interests, and the occasional unreasonableness of other States. . . . The unpleasantness of mob government has never before been exemplified so conspicuously, for it never before has worked upon so large a scene.

One does not, of course, have to accept the Tory accent to recognize the validity of Bagehot's analysis. Simply because Americans by the middle of the nineteenth century suffered from unrestricted liberty, they were increasingly unable to arrive at reasoned, independent judgments upon the problems that faced their society. The permanent revolution that was America had freed its citizens from the bonds of prescription and custom but had left them leaderless. Inevitably the reverse side of the coin of individualism is conformity. Huddling together in their loneliness, they sought only to escape their freedom. Fads, fashions, and crazes swept the country. Religious revivalism reached a new peak in the 1850's. Hysterical fears and paranoid suspicions marked this shift of Americans to "other-directedness." Never was there a field so fertile before the propagandist, the agitator, the extremist.

III

THESE DANGEROUSLY DIVISIVE TENDENCIES in American society did not, of course, go unnoticed. Tocqueville and other

European observers were aware of the perils of social atomization and predicted that, under shock, the Union might be divided. Nor were all Americans indifferent to the drift of events. Repeatedly in the Middle Period conservative statesmen tried to check the widespread social disorganization. Henry Clay, for example, attempted to revive the idea of the national interest, superior to local and individual interests, by binding together the sections in his American System: the West should produce the nation's food; the South its staples; and the East its manufactures. The chief purpose of Daniel Webster's great patriotic orations was to stimulate a national feeling based on shared traditions, values, and beliefs. Taking as his twin maxims "The best authority for the support of a particular provision in government is experience . . ." and "Because a thing has been wrongly done, it does not therefore follow that it can now be undone . . . ," Webster tried to preserve the Union from shocks and rapid change. John C. Calhoun, too, argued for uniting "the most opposite and conflicting interests . . . into one common attachment to the country" through protecting the rights of minorities. With suitable guarantees to vested sectional interests (notably to slavery), Calhoun predicted that "the community would become a unity, by becoming a common center of attachment of all its parts. And hence, instead of faction, strife, and struggle for party ascendancy, there would be patriotism, nationality, harmony, and a struggle only for supremacy in promoting the common good of the whole."

Nor did conservative statesmanship die with the generation of Webster, Clay, and Calhoun. Down to the very outbreak of the Civil War old Whigs like John Jordan Crittenden, John Bell, and Edward Everett argued for adjustment of sectional claims to the national interests. Abraham Lincoln, another former Whig, tried to check the majoritarianism of his fellow countrymen by harking back to the Declaration of Independence, which he termed the "sheet anchor of our principles." In the doctrine that all men are created equal Lincoln found justification for his belief that there were some rights upon which no majority, however large or however democratic, might infringe. Majority rule, he maintained, could no more justify the extension of slavery to the territories than majority rule could disenfranchise the Irish, or the Catholics, or the laboring men of America. Soberly he warned that in a country like America, where there was no prescriptive right, the future of democratic government depended upon the willingness of its citizens to admit moral limits to their political powers.

None of these attempts to curb the tyranny of the majority was successful; all went too strongly against the democratic current of the age. American society was changing so rapidly that there was no true conservative group or interest to which a statesman could safely appeal. Webster, it is clear, would have preferred to find his following among yeoman farmers holding approximately equal wealth; instead he was obliged to rely upon the banking, manufacturing, and speculative interests of the Northeast, the hard, grasping, *arriviste* element of society, a group that had itself risen through the democratic process. These special interests used Webster to secure tariffs, banking acts, and internal improvement legislation favorable to themselves, but they selfishly dropped him when he talked of subordinating their local particularism to the broad national interest.

Similarly, Calhoun sought a conservative backing in the plantation aristocracy, the same aristocracy that in a previous generation had produced George Washington, James Madison, and John Marshall. But while Calhoun prated of a Greek democracy, in which all white men, freed by Negro slavery of the burdens of menial labor, could deliberate upon statesmanlike solutions to the nation's problems, the conservative aristocracy upon which his theories depended was vanishing. Political and economic leadership moved from Virginia, first to South Carolina, then to Mississippi. The educated, cosmopolitan plantation owners of the 1780's disappeared; in their place emerged the provincial Southron, whose sentiments were precisely expressed by an up-country South Carolinian: "I'll give you my notion of things; I go first for Greenville, then for Greenville District, then for the up-country, then for South Carolina, then for the South, then for the United States; and after that I don't go for anything. I've no use for Englishmen, Turks and Chinese." These slavemasters of the new cotton kingdom endorsed Calhoun and his doctrines so long as their own vested interests were being protected; after that, they ignored his conservative philosophy.

Possibly in time this disorganized society might have evolved a genuinely conservative solution for its problems, but time ran against it. At a stage when the United States was least capable of enduring shock, the nation was obliged to undergo a series of crises, largely triggered by the physical expansion of the country. The annexation of Texas, the war with Mexico, and the settlement of California and Oregon posed inescapable problems of organizing and governing this new empire. Something had to be done, yet any action was bound to arouse local, sectional hostilities. Similarly in 1854 it was necessary to organize the Great Plains territory, but, as Stephen A. Douglas painfully learned, organizing it without slavery alienated the South, organizing it with slavery offended the North, and organizing it under popular sovereignty outraged both sections.

As if these existential necessities did not impose enough strains upon a disorganized society, well-intentioned individuals insisted upon adding others. The quite unnecessary shock administered by the Dred Scott decision in 1857 is a case in point; justices from the antislavery North and the proslavery South, determined to settle the slavery issue once and for all, produced opinions that in fact settled nothing but only led to further alienation and embitterment. Equally unnecessary, of course, was the far ruder shock that crazy John Brown and his little band administered two years later when they decided to solve the nation's problems by taking the law into their own hands at Harpers Ferry.

These crises that afflicted the United States in the 1850's were not in themselves calamitous experiences. Revisionist historians have correctly pointed out how little was actually at stake: slavery did not go into New Mexico or Arizona; Kansas, after having been opened to the peculiar institution for six years, had only two Negro slaves; the Dred Scott decision declared an already repealed law unconstitutional; John Brown's raid had no significant support in the North and certainly roused no visible enthusiasm among Southern

Negroes. When compared to crises that other nations have resolved without great discomfort, the true proportions of these exaggerated disturbances appear.

But American society in the 1850's was singularly ill equipped to meet any shocks, however weak. It was a society so new and so disorganized that its nerves were rawly exposed. It was, as Henry James noted, a land that had "no sovereign, no court, no personal loyalty, no aristocracy, no church, no clergy, no army, no diplomatic service, no country gentlemen, no palaces, no castles, nor manors, nor old country houses, nor parsonages, nor thatched cottages, nor ivied ruins; no cathedrals, nor abbeys, nor little Norman churches; no great universities nor public schools . . . ; no literature, no novels, no museums, no pictures, no political society" — in short, it had no resistance to strain. The very similarity of the social processes that affected all sections of the country — the expansion of the frontier, the rise of the city, the exploitation of great natural wealth — produced not cohesion but individualism. The structure of the American political system impeded the appearance of conservative statesmanship, and the rapidity of the crises in the 1850's prevented conservatism from crystallizing. The crises themselves were not world-shaking, nor did they inevitably produce war. They were, however, the chisel strokes that revealed the fundamental flaws in the block of marble, flaws that stemmed from an excess of democracy.

FIVE

Education Defective:
Lincoln's Preparation for Greatness

IN 1858, when Charles Lanman was compiling his *Dictionary of Congress*, he wrote to all present and past members of the House of Representatives and the Senate for biographical information. Most responded with full curricula vitae, detailing their accomplishments in public and private life. Many boasted of their superior education and training for high office. Of the Illinois delegation to the Thirtieth Congress (1847–49), for example, Senator Sidney Breese announced that he had attended Hamilton College and had graduated from Union College; Representative John Wentworth reported that he had a Dartmouth degree; and Orlando Ficklen and William Richardson proudly claimed to be products of Transylvania University.

Abraham Lincoln, who was also a member of that delegation, sent Lanman a characteristically terse seven-line autobiographical statement, giving only the place and date of his birth, identifying himself as a lawyer by profession, stating that he had been a captain of volunteers in the Black Hawk War, and mentioning that he had served four terms in the Illinois legislature and one in the lower house of Congress. But the most interesting line in his brief autobiography was his flat notation: "Education defective."

I

IN LETTERS WRITTEN IN THE 1850's, at a time when Lincoln was becoming politically prominent and there were repeated requests for biographical information, he added a few more details about his education. He had no distinct memories of his Kentucky schools. A relative remembered that he attended them "more as Company for his Sister than with the expectation that he would learn Much." His first teacher was one Zachariah Riney, about whom almost nothing is known except that he was a Catholic. The second was Caleb Hazel, who, according to a contemporary, "could perhaps teach spelling, reading and indifferent writing and perhaps could cipher to the rule of three [i.e., ratio and proportion], but had no other qualifications of a teacher, except large size and bodily strength to thrash any boy or youth that came to his school." Abraham probably mastered the alphabet before his family left Kentucky, but he did not yet know how to write.

In Indiana there was initially little opportunity for further education. During the first hard year while the family was getting settled on Little Pigeon Creek there was no time for schooling, and then Nancy Hanks Lincoln died and the family was demoralized. But when Thomas Lincoln remarried, his new wife felt strongly about education and sent the children to a school that Andrew Crawford had opened about a mile from the Lincoln cabin. They attended for a term of perhaps three months; Abraham was about eleven years old. During the next two years, after Crawford gave up teaching, there was no school in the neighborhood. When James Swaney opened another one, it was about four miles from the Lincoln cabin, and Abraham, who had chores to perform, could attend only sporadically. The next year, for most of a term, he went to a school taught by Azel W. Dorsey.

With that, at the age of fifteen, his formal education came to an end. "The agregate of all his schooling," he recalled, "did not amount to one year."

11

LINCOLN WAS SCORNFUL of these "schools, so called" that he had attended, however briefly, and in many ways they merited his low opinion. He grew up, it will be remembered, in the darkest period in the history of American education. Even in New England, where the Puritan spirit had once required each town to establish a public school, education languished; it would be another fifteen years before Horace Mann and his allies forced the reorganization of public education in Massachusetts and other states. Outside of New England the situation was even worse, and most states had no public school system. The Northwest Ordinance had carefully set aside public lands to support education, but most of the fund was squandered. When Indiana was admitted to the Union in 1816, its constitution required that free public education be made available to all, but no money was ever appropriated for schools.

The schools that did exist were proprietary efforts. A self-described teacher secured subscriptions of $2.00 or $2.50 from the parents of children in his neighborhood, built or rented a building, and opened shop. The physical facilities were, at best, primitive. Azel Dorsey's school, for example, was a one-room cabin, "built of unhewn logs, and had 'holes for windows,' in which 'greased paper' served for glass. The roof was just high enough for a man to stand erect." The floor was made of split logs, as were the students' seats. Heat came from a huge fireplace at one end of the room. (By way of contrast, Swaney's schoolhouse had two chimneys and was accounted palatial.)

Teaching methods were dictated by the absence of black-boards, chalk, and textbooks and by the scarcity of paper. These were often called "blab" schools, because the teacher, holding the only copy of the text in his hand, would read a line aloud, and all the children would repeat it in chorus. It goes without saying that these schools were ungraded.

Anyone who wished could set up as a teacher; there was no method of certification and no requirement of credentials. Thinking back on those who taught him, Lincoln remembered that "no qualification was ever required of a teacher beyond '*reading, writin, and cipherin,*' to the Rule of Three. If a straggler supposed to understand latin, happened to sojourn in the neighborhood, he was looked up as a wizzard."

III

BEFORE FULLY ENDORSING Lincoln's negative verdict on these Kentucky and Indiana schools, it might be well to look a bit more closely at the education they offered. After all, if they were so hopelessly bad it is hard to see how they could have produced an Abraham Lincoln.

Lincoln's statement that he attended these schools for a total of only about a year is accurate, but to evaluate it we need to remember that school terms in the early nineteenth century were brief. Even in New York State as late as 1840 the average school term lasted only twenty days. On the frontier—where distances were greater, where travel was impossible during the winter, and where the children's labor was needed during the farming season— they were even shorter. It is reasonable to calculate that Lincoln's "agregate of one year" in school totaled about six of these brief terms. At that time this was considered a full common-school education— and it was a great deal more than many children received. In Indiana alone, with a population of 300,000 children at this time, it is estimated that 50,000 received no education and were illiterate.

During these short terms the schools offered alert students a sufficient mastery of basic language tools. *Dilworth's Spelling-Book,* which Abraham and his sister, Sarah, had begun to use in Kentucky, provided an introduction to spelling and grammar. Starting with the alphabet and Arabic and Roman numerals, it proceeded to words of two letters, then three letters, and finally four letters. From this the students began to construct sentences, like "No man may put off the law of God." *Dilworth's* then discussed more advanced subjects, and the final sections included prose and verse selections, some accompanied by crude woodcuts—perhaps the first pictures that Abraham Lincoln ever saw.

He and his classmates also studied from Noah Webster's "Old Blue-Back" Spelling Book, a copy of which Sarah Bush Johnston, his stepmother, had brought from Kentucky. It contained valuable "Precepts Concerning Social Relations," advising how husbands and wives, parents and children, brothers and sisters should behave toward one another. Abraham Lincoln internalized some of these, like the maxim of humility: "The humble man has few or no enemies. Every one loves him and is ready to do him good." In his very first race for public office, in 1832, he introduced himself to the voters with: "I was born and have ever remained in the most humble walks of life." On at least thirty-five other public occasions prior to 1860 he referred to himself as "humble."

The best evidence that Lincoln's schoolmasters were not so lamentably deficient as he portrayed them is the passionate interest he developed in reading outside of his schoolwork. This cannot have been due to the influence of his parents, because Thomas Lincoln could read only a little, and with difficulty, while his stepmother was illiterate. According to his cousin Dennis F. Hanks the boy was "a Constant I m[a]y say Stubborn reader." Another cousin, John Hanks, who worked in the field with Abraham, recalled that when he returned to the cabin, "he would go to the Cupboard—Snatch a piece of Corn bread—take down a book—Sit down on a chair—Cock his legs up as high as his head and read." "He read all the books he could lay his hands on," his stepmother agreed. "He read diligently—studied in the day time . . . went to bed Early—got up Early and then read."

There were not many books in pioneer southern Indiana, but Lincoln read everything he could find. He spent hours reading the Bible that his stepmother had brought from Kentucky, and he committed long passages to memory. In his public statements of later years he would make more references to the Bible than has any other American President. When his father brought him a copy of *Pilgrim's Progress*, Abraham was so delighted that "his eyes sparkled, and that day he could not eat, and that night he could not sleep." He memorized much of it and often quoted it as President. He read Aesop's *Fables* over and over again; decades later he would make powerful use of the moral of Aesop's fable about the Lion and the Four Bulls: "A kingdom divided against itself cannot stand."

Lincoln's early schooling gave him a lifelong interest in the structure and use of language. After he left his family and moved to New Salem, Illinois, he decided that he needed to make a more formal study of the subject, and, learning that a farmer named John C. Vance had a copy of Kirkham's grammar, he willingly walked six miles into the country to borrow it. He then set himself systematically to mastering this detailed text, committing large segments to memory. Then he asked his friends to test him and, when challenged to provide a definition of a verb, could recite: "a VERB is a word which signifies to BE, to DO, or to SUFFER; as I *am*, I *rule*; I *am ruled*."

I V

SIMILARLY, it is easy to underestimate the training that Lincoln received in basic mathematics, but fortunately we have a record of what he learned. Because paper was scarce on the frontier, he often had to do his homework on boards and, his stepmother recalled, "when the board would get too black he would shave it off with a drawing knife and go on again." Eventually he found a few sheets of paper, which he sewed together to form a little notebook, in which he wrote down his more advanced problems and the solutions to them that he had previously worked out.

The several sheets of his notebook that have been preserved tell a great deal about Lincoln and about his teachers. Careful research by historians of mathematics shows that the problems he was assigned did not come from any single textbook but, instead, were drawn from at least four sources, the most important of which were Thomas Dilworth's *The Teacher's Assistant* and Stephen Pike's book of the same title. Clearly the stereotype of a teacher rattling off assignments from a single textbook, of which he held the only copy, must be incorrect. Probably Lincoln's instructors taught mathematics from handmade manuals, from which perhaps they themselves had learned.

The textbooks may have been primitive, but Lincoln's handmade notebook shows the instruction was not. In his notebook he carefully recorded tables of weights and measures, methods for calculating simple and compound interest, together with discounts, and sample problems over which he struggled. He did not find it easy to solve problems involving ratio and proportion, though he found the correct answer to questions like: "If 3 oz of Silver cost 17S what will 48 oz cost?" But he had no difficulty with complicated calculations involving multiplication (like 34,5867,834 x 24,423) and long division (such as 4,375,701 divided by 2,432).

Once again the real test of Lincoln's training in mathematics came after he left Indiana. On moving to New Salem he discovered that one of the few ways he could make a living was by becoming a surveyor. Knowing nothing of that art but drawing on his training in arithmetic, he secured some basic texts and set himself to mastering the principles of trigonometry and their practical application to surveying. Soon he was one of the most careful and successful surveyors in the field. He was, for example, the principal surveyor in locating a public road from the Sangamon River through New Salem on toward Jacksonville. He laid out the plans for the towns of New Boston, Bath, Petersburg, and Huron. So meticulous was his work that, as a resident of Athens, Illinois, recalled: "Mr. Lincoln had the monopoly of finding the lines, and when there was any dispute arose among the Settlers Mr Lincoln's Compass and chain always settled the matter satisfactorily."

V

IF THIS ANALYSIS IS VALID, it is puzzling that Abraham Lincoln repeatedly minimized, and even denigrated, his schooling. The obvious explanation is that he did so for political purposes. It helps to remember—however improbable it may sound today—that early in his political career, when he sought the Whig nomination for Congress in 1843, Lincoln's political enemies portrayed him as "the candidate of pride, wealth, and aristocratic family distinctions." His recent marriage to Mary Todd, the daughter of a wealthy, slave-owning Kentucky merchant, linked him to the upper-class Whig junto that ruled Springfield society and politics. So did Lincoln's increasing prosperity as a lawyer. He fought hard to convince his supporters that at heart he was still the "friendless, uneducated, penniless boy" who had come to Illinois twelve years earlier, but he failed to win the nomination.

The defeat taught him a lesson. Thereafter Lincoln consistently presented himself to the public as a simple, industrious laboring man, the untutored child of the frontier, who had risen solely through his own exertions. Recognizing the importance of appearing to be a self-made man (to use the phrase that Henry Clay had recently coined), Lincoln downplayed his education. He learned almost to boast of his ignorance. During his 1858 debates with Stephen A. Douglas, in which he demonstrated his superb ability as a rhetorician and orator, he announced in a self-deprecating tone: "I am not master of language. I have not a fine education: I am not capable of entering into a disquisition upon dialectics, as I believe you call it." A little later, in a third-person autobiography, written while he was running for President, he seemed to take pride in his defective education: "He was never in a college or Academy as a student and never inside of a college of academy building till since he had a law-license."

Clearly by minimizing his educational accomplishments Lincoln was building what Richard Hofstadter called his "self-made myth," but the tone and context of Lincoln's animadversions about his schooling suggest that there was more at work here than political calculation. He stressed the primitive conditions in southern Indiana when he was growing up, "a wild region, with many bears and other wild animals still in the wood," where, he remarked scornfully, there was "absolutely nothing to excite ambition for education." Often his comments on his schooling were connected with condescending remarks about his father. Thomas Lincoln, Abraham explained in an 1859 autobiographical sketch, was "litterally without education"; he grew up "a wandering laboring boy," who "never did more in the way of writing than to bunglingly sign his own name."

The bitterness of such remarks suggests that Lincoln was lamenting not merely the primitive schools he had attended but, more broadly, the way he had been brought up. As Bernard Bailyn points out, in the early day of the republic, before public schools became widespread, it was generally accepted that the education of a child was the obligation, first, of his family, second, of his church, and third, of the society in which he grew up. Abraham felt that none of these had helped him. From Thomas Lincoln he learned only the craft of carpentry—which he despised—and the heavy labor of primitive farming. From his mother he inherited only an abiding sense of loss at her early death, which may have colored his deep melancholy. His stepmother, though warm and affectionate, had no education. As for the churches, the primitive evangelical sects of southern Indiana made no attempt to promote education; indeed, some were hostile to learning. And there was no "society" in which Abraham Lincoln grew up; "neighbors" were settlers who lived two or three miles apart, separated by unbroken forest. Except for the intermittent religious services and the sporadic school terms there was no community life.

Lincoln hardly noticed his want of education in the frontier community of New Salem, but after 1837 when he moved to more socially pretentious Springfield he began to realize how much he differed from most of his aspiring contemporaries. As he wrote to one young woman at this time, he did not go to church, because he was unsure how to behave. He welcomed social invitations, but he did not know how to dress or act. Nobody had ever taught him that it was inappropriate to come to a dance wearing his rough Conestoga boots or corrected him when he disrupted a party by exclaiming: "Oh boys how clean these girls look." His future sister-in-law later remarked that he had no idea how to converse with women.

Marriage to Mary Todd, who not merely had an excellent education but was trained in the best finishing school in Lexington, Kentucky, helped remedy some of these deficiencies but at the same time made Lincoln conscious of his limitations. In many ways Mary was of enormous help to him socially. For instance, she made a point of seeing that he was well and carefully dressed—or as well dressed as any man, six feet and four inches tall, and built like a scarecrow, could be. But there were limits to her influence. She was unable to interest him in current literature; the names of Charles Dickens and William Makepeace Thackeray, of Nathaniel Hawthorne, Herman Melville and Walt Whitman do not appear in his letters or papers. Indeed, Mary could not persuade her husband to read any fiction. He once started *Ivanhoe*, he said, but he never could finish it.

Lincoln's two years in the House of Representatives (1847–49) made him even more aware of his limited education. He was not so much impressed by his colleagues' ability to quote from the Latin, and occasionally the Greek, classics as he was by the clarity and elegance with which they presented their arguments. On his return to Springfield he told his law partner, Herndon, that he felt "a certain lack of discipline—a want of mental training and method," and characteristically he set about making up his deficit. Believing, as did most of his contemporaries, that mental faculties were like muscles, which could be strengthened by rigorous exercise, he secured a copy of Euclid's principles of geometry and with determination began to work through the theorems and problems. With quiet pride he reported in 1860 that he had "studied and nearly mastered the Six-books of Euclid."

VI

IN TIME LINCOLN CAME TO RECOGNIZE that he had exaggerated the importance of his educational backwardness. An unconscious indication of his changing views appeared as early as 1852 in his eulogy on Henry Clay, his "beau idea of a statesman." Describing Clay's formal education as "comparatively limited," Lincoln noted that Clay "added something to his education during the greater part of his whole life." Then he went on to generalize in a statement that applied even more to himself than to Clay: his "lack of a more perfect early education, however it may be regretted generally, teaches at least one profitable lesson; it teaches that in this country, one can scarcely be so poor, but that, if he *will*, he *can* acquire sufficient education to get through the world respectably."

Lincoln's respectable education—however defective in a formal sense—served him well in the White House. As President he insisted that intelligence was more important than schooling. He took a certain pleasure in overruling Secretary of War Edwin M. Stanton, who objected that one of his nominees had only limited schooling: "I personally wish Jacob R. Freese, of New Jersey to be appointed a Colonel . . . and this regardless of whether he can tell the exact shade of Julius Caesar's hair." At times he even made a virtue of his lack of schooling. Late in the war, when Lincoln and Secretary of State William H. Seward met with three leading Confederates to discuss possible peace terms, he told the Southerners that he could not agree to an armistice so long as they continued to bear arms against the United States government. When one of them objected that in the past governments had often entered into agreements with rebels and that Charles I of England had frequently negotiated with those who were fighting against him, Lincoln responded tartly: "I do not profess to be posted in history. On all such matters I will turn you over to Seward. All I distinctly recollect about the case of Charles I, is, that he lost his head in the end."

Such remarks suggest a man who was, finally, at peace with himself. In the White House, where he had daily to take the measure of men like Charles Sumner and Salmon P. Chase, who were far more learned than he could ever be, Lincoln came to understand that his education had better prepared him than any of his rivals to lead the nation through a great war. Once he reached this conclusion, he did not try to conceal it. As John Hay, his private secretary, remarked: "It is absurd to call him a modest man. No great man was ever modest. It was his intellectual arrogance and unconscious assumption of superiority that men like Chase and Sumner could never forgive."

SIX

Herndon and Mary Lincoln

I

ANN RUTLEDGE WAS the only woman Lincoln ever loved. But after his removal to Springfield he was trapped by the ambitious and aggressive Mary Todd into a promise of marriage. The appointed day came, the feast was prepared, the guests were waiting, the bride was decked out in her finery—but the groom did not appear. Lincoln felt he could not marry this woman he did not love. Later, however, consideration of his plighted honor forced him to go through with the ceremony, and Mary Todd became Mrs. Abraham Lincoln. From that day in November 1842 Lincoln's home life was a domestic hell. Mary Lincoln made it so unpleasant for him that he was forced to interest himself in politics. He was driven from home into the White House.

Most people believe that this is the story of Abraham Lincoln's married life. Many can cite one story or another to "prove" their point. These ideas have become so widespread as to form an accepted part of a great national tradition, and the recent publication of two admirable defenses of Mary Lincoln has done little to upset these stereotypes. Yet they are 100 percent incorrect.

There is a fascination in tracing this legend back to its origin and in seeing how it developed and grew. The Ann Rutledge story, the defaulting-bridegroom incident, and the anecdotes of married strife all go back to one man, to Abraham Lincoln's law partner and biographer, William Henry Herndon. This man Herndon was in many ways as interesting as Lincoln himself. A curiously divided personality, he was on the one hand a fighting idealist, a champion of causes, a man of drums and trumpets; on the other, he was a man of the common people, of barnyard vulgarity, who knew men's talk about drinking and cockfights and horses and women. Born in Kentucky in 1818 (just twelve days after Mary Todd saw the light in cultured Lexington), he was early taken by his father to pioneer in Illinois, in the wild Sangamon country. In the 1820's Herndon's father moved to the hamlet of Springfield, where he opened the Indian Queen, the first tavern in the community. Here young Billy got to know the leaders of the ambitious village, learned to laugh at their jokes and to understand their talk of politics. Here, too, he acquired that taste for liquor which was so tragically to blight his later years.

But there was more to this youth than the hanger-on at the tavern. He did well in the Springfield schools, and his proud father sent him at an almost unheard-of expense to attend the preparatory division of Illinois College. He had one exciting year at Jacksonville. He dimly saw vistas of sweeping fields of knowledge; from the library, where he was permitted to borrow two small volumes or one large book each week, he caught an insatiable appetite for reading. But at the end of the year he failed in mathematics and was not allowed to register for college courses.

Back in Springfield, Herndon clerked for Joshua Speed and slept with Speed, Abraham Lincoln, and another clerk in the big room above the store. Then he married and began raising a family. And, most important of all, he started studying law with the two best lawyers the Illinois capital could offer—Logan and Lincoln. Lincoln wrote that Herndon was "a laborious, studious young man, . . . far better informed on almost all subjects than I have been." It was not surprising, then, that Lincoln in 1844 should choose this promising student for his new law partner. The association thus formed lasted without interruption until Lincoln went to Washington, and in 1865 the Lincoln & Herndon shingle still creaked over the office door. Herndon became a competent lawyer and did the "book work" for the firm. In politics, too, he helped—so well that Springfield newspapers called him "Lincoln's man Friday."

Herndon was an eager and earnest young man. There was something almost pathetic in the way he sought knowledge. He loved books, the deeper and more "philosophic" the better. He was fascinated by the rolling periods of grandiloquent oratory and by the lofty abstractions of metaphysicians. He read Kant and Comte, Holyoke and Hobbes. He reveled in speculations of the more abstruse sort: What is law? What is the nature of the mind? What is the ultimate source of knowledge? His speculative turn was stimulated by a long series of letters that he exchanged with Theodore Parker, the Boston Unitarian radical. Herndon poured out his soul to this man; he told him everything—of politics and philosophy and the slavery controversy and the law office, and sometimes of his partner, "Mr. Lincoln."

It is important to understand how Herndon went about his almost desperate search for Truth. Truth was not something that could be found in books, not even the Bible; nor was Truth spoken by the Sage alone. Given a Divine Providence and a soul in the individual man, it was the belief of the Transcendentalists—Parker, Emerson, Thoreau, for all of whom Herndon had an almost painful admiration—that Truth could be found by introspection. If you wished to explain a man's actions, look to your own soul, where you would find identical motives reflected. All men operate on the same laws, and these laws can explain any human behavior.

There were many problems that Herndon wanted to solve. He sought to know the laws of the "All-All' and of "zo-ophyte & man." He was puzzled by the secrets of the winds and of the hibernacle surrounding the tiny leaf bud, the mystery of the sun and the rain. But there were human problems facing him, too. One of them was his office mate. Herndon could never quite figure Lincoln out. He behaved queerly—i.e., differently from Herndon. He seemed to drip melancholy as he walked, but his fits of deep depression would alternate with gusty outbreaks of humor. There must be something wrong with this man.

In groping for an explanation, Herndon did not go far. He

promptly concluded that the trouble with Lincoln was Mrs. Lincoln. Herndon had never liked Mary Todd. When she first came to Illinois he had met her at a ball given by Colonel Allen. This youth back from college had danced with the belle, and, thinking to compliment her, had informed Mary that she waltzed with the grace of a serpent. Miss Todd, never distinguished for a sense of humor, had flashed back: "Mr. Herndon, comparison to a serpent is rather severe irony, especially to a newcomer"—and she left him on the dance floor. Neither ever forgot the scene. Twenty years later, when Herndon visited the Lincolns at the White House, he wrote a friend that Mrs. Lincoln was becoming more "eccentric" every day; that she had, to his personal knowledge, made Lincoln's life desolate since they were married. Of course, it was not all friction between them, for a wife cannot completely snub her husband's partner. Mary Lincoln occasionally borrowed small sums from Herndon while her husband was out on the circuit, and after Lincoln's death she spoke graciously to Herndon of "my beloved husband's, *truly*, affectionate regard for *you*." So far the amenities of life would carry her, but not further; she never invited Herndon to have a meal at her home.

It was in this atmosphere of mutual dislike that Herndon did his thinking about his partner's melancholy and his sudden moods. By a comparison with his own home life, he could easily tell what was wrong. Herndon hated to spend a night away from his family; Lincoln would go off sometimes for months on the circuit without returning to Springfield. It was obvious, thought Herndon, that his partner's home life was unhappy. Herndon would invite a casual acquaintance to dinner without giving his wife any notice; Lincoln had guests only when Mary specially asked them. It must be, said Herndon, that Mrs. Lincoln was of a shrewish and inhospitable temperament. When the Herndon children came to the law office—which was not often—they were given law books and told to sit quietly on a bench; when the Lincoln boys were brought in by their father, Herndon wrote, "they would take down the books from the shelves—scatter them over the floor—mash up gold pens—

spill the ink all over the floor." Clearly, Herndon thought, the Lincolns lacked discipline.

Before Lincoln's death Herndon kept his views largely to himself, but in 1865 he decided to write a biography of the man he had known so well and at the same time so little. It was to be a subjective, personal biography explaining why Lincoln acted and thought as he did. One of the springs of Lincoln's nature Herndon found in gathering reminiscences from New Salem acquaintances. From twisted recollections of events more than thirty years past, from hearsay and gossip, from inferences as to what must have been, and from speculations as to what might have been, he wove the fabric of the Ann Rutledge story, which he spread before the Springfield people in a long lecture in 1866. In lush periods of purple phrases he told his fellow citizens that Ann was the only woman Lincoln had ever loved, that as late as 1860 he had still cherished his affection for her alone.

Mrs. Lincoln, her sons, and her friends were outraged. It was, it should be remembered, a romantic age, this mid-Victorian period when ladies had limbs and not legs, when marriage meant—or was supposed to mean—invariable connubial bliss, when debunking was not dreamed of. The true lady, etiquette books of the day pronounced, should be mentioned in the newspapers only twice—when she married and when she died; if her name occurred in print at any other time, a male relative ought to visit the editor with a shotgun. Mrs. Lincoln was a proud, sensitive lady, the more so now that she was alone in the world. She retaliated upon Herndon by declaring that her husband had always thought of him as a drunkard and a wastrel. And Herndon came back with a blistering excoriation: Mrs. Lincoln was a liar, subject to spasmodic fits of insanity. From then on it was open warfare. Year after year went by, and Herndon became more and more bitter. Age and drink cast a cloud over his brilliant mind and made trivial details stand out with sharp poignancy. Mrs. Lincoln, he now thought, was the "she wolf of this section," "soured . . . gross . . . material—avaricious—insolent," "a tigress," "terribly aristocratic . . . and haughty," "as cold as a chunk of ice." He brooded over real and imagined slights and stirred up his memory. Twenty years after Lincoln's death he concluded that Mary Lincoln was *"the female wild cat of the age."*

II

IT IS ONLY BY DISCOUNTING these belated recollections and garbled introspections that one can hope to arrive at a true picture of Mary Lincoln. Herndon assiduously collected backstairs gossip about Mrs. Lincoln and spread it as truth. He did not consciously misinterpret facts, for he was really determined to "do justice" to Mrs. Lincoln. But he was eager to accept stories that fitted in with his preconceived ideas. Any thinking person will realize how difficult it is to remember correctly the back-fence gossip of twenty to forty years earlier, even assuming that the gossip was ever correct in the first place.

By following strictly contemporary accounts one gets a different view of Mrs. Lincoln. When Miss Mary Todd came to Springfield in 1839 to make her home with her sister, Mrs. Ninian W. Edwards, she came as a belle, as an interesting and attractive young woman destined to be the center of social life and gaiety. The Todds were a proud and distinguished family in Kentucky, numbering two governors, a couple of Cabinet members, and a score of less distinguished officials as close relatives. It was the Todds, together with the Crittendens and the Clays, who set the social tone for Lexington. Yet the Todd name carried with it a less desirable heritage, too — a sort of mental taint, a tendency toward abnormally intense personalities, ill adapted to severe crises or harsh shocks. The medical record shows that Mary Todd's own brother became a mental case.

But all this was in the future. For Miss Todd was a brilliant addition to Springfield society in the 1830's. She had been well educated at Mme. Mentelle's, both in English fundamentals and in French, which she read fluently. She could write a gracious and well-expressed letter. She could dance and hold sprightly conversa-

tions with men. She was a born coquette. When life with her stepmother in Kentucky became unendurable, it was natural that she
should visit her Springfield sister, for here she might find an attractive husband and a home. Women are always at a premium in a
frontier society, and it is not surprising that the Edwards house in
the winters of 1839 and 1840 was a center of gaiety. There were balls
and sleigh rides and excursions and parties. Half a dozen young
men danced in attendance upon the new queen—James C. Conkling, Joshua Speed, Stephen A. Douglas, and a gawky young
lawyer called Abraham Lincoln. Mary was excited and delighted by
such attentions. In a letter of the time a friend described her as "the
very creature of excitement," who "never enjoy[ed] herself more
than when in society and surrounded by a company of merry
friends."

"Mary," as her niece remembered her, "although not strictly
beautiful, was more than pretty. She had a broad, white forehead,
eyebrows sharply but delicately marked, a straight nose, short upper
lip, and an expressive mouth curling into an adorable, slow-coming
smile that brought dimples into her cheeks and glinted in her long-
lashed, blue eyes." Observers noted her "Plump round figure," her
"lovely complexion," her "soft brown hair." One of the clearest pictures of Mary Todd at this time comes from Herndon himself: "of a
short build—chunky—compact and about of the average height—
and waid [*sic*] ... about 130 pounds ... haughtily dignified—
moved easily ... a fine conversation[li]st—witty and sometimes
terribly sarcastic ... intelligent—quick—intuitive." Others also
noted Miss Todd's sharp tongue, even while admitting her charm.
She could be gracious, but she could also flash out with an
ungovernable temper—possibly a reflection of her lack of early
home training.

She was ambitious, intelligently so. She came to find a husband, and she intended to make a good choice. Half laughingly,
Mary said that she was going to marry the man who would become
President of the United States. It is not hard to understand why she
rejected one widower, referring to his motherless children as "two
sweet little objections." The extent of Stephen A. Douglas's atten-

tions has probably been exaggerated, but he was very often in the Edwards parlor. But it was Abraham Lincoln with whom she finally fell in love. It must have been an amusing courtship—for an outsider. Awkward and rough and a little embarrassed in the presence of ladies, Lincoln would sit and listen fascinated by Mary's prattle, but he could not carry on the conversation himself. Friends advised Mary against the match, pointing out Lincoln's poor prospects and his even poorer present. Exactly what happened during those winter months of 1840-41 is not clear, but apparently there was an engagement of some sort, or at least an understanding.

The commonly accepted story, started by Herndon and spread by fiction writers, is that the two were to be married. To quote Herndon's version: "The time fixed for the marriage was the first day in January, 1841. Careful preparations for the happy occasion were made at the Edwards mansion. The house underwent the customary renovation; . . . the supper [was] prepared, and the guests invited. The latter assembled on the evening in question, and awaited in expectant pleasure the interesting ceremony of marriage. The bride, bedecked in veil and silken gown, and nervously toying with the flowers in her hair, sat in the adjoining room. Nothing was lacking but the groom." Hours passed, and Lincoln failed to appear. The wedding plans were abandoned, and the guests quietly departed.

This is not the place to examine this wedding story in detail. It is enough to realize that the whole episode was created from self-contradictory reminiscences given years after the event; that no contemporary letter by Mary Todd, Lincoln, or their friends mentions a projected marriage for the couple; that Lincoln did not take out a marriage license in 1840; and that Springfield gossips did not spread the tale until after Lincoln's death.

But if there was no deserted bride, no waiting guests or garlanded house, there was certainly a major emotional crisis about this time. Lincoln referred to the day as "that fatal first of January. '41," and he considered himself "the most miserable man living." "If what I feel were equally distributed to the whole human family," he wrote disconsolately, "there would not be one cheerful face on the earth." A friend remarked that "he is reduced and emaciated in appearance and seems scarcely to possess strength enough to speak above a whisper," and laughingly called Lincoln a "poor, hapless simple swain who loved most true but was not loved again."

Mary Todd, though she carried on the round of parties and entertainment, was none too happy either. Lincoln, she wrote to a bosom companion, "deems me unworthy of notice, as I have not met *him* in the gay world for months . . . others were as seldom gladdened by his presence as my humble self, yet I would that . . . he would once more resume his station in Society, that 'Richard should be himself again,' much, much happiness would it afford me."

The best reconstruction that can now be made of the whole tangle is as follows: About the first of January 1841, Lincoln, realizing his poverty and doubting his ability to make a sensitive and cultured woman happy, asked to be released from his engagement. Mary consented, though letting it be known that she would consider the question still open. Thus the crisis passed.

It was not until nearly two years later that their marriage actually took place. During that time Lincoln was comforted by the knowledge that the marriage of his friend Joshua Speed was successful. He was also rising to a more secure financial position as one of the leading lawyers in Springfield. The estranged couple was brought together through the agency of Mrs. Simeon Francis, a common friend, and the engagement was renewed. There was no public announcement, for Mary said "that the world, woman and man, were uncertain and slippery and that it was best to keep the secret courtship from all eyes and ears." Some months later, on November 4, 1842, the two were married.

The Lincolns at first stayed at the Globe Tavern, where they got room and board for four dollars a week. It was here that their first son, Robert Todd, was born. In 1846 a second child, Edward Baker, came, and the same year Lincoln was elected to Congress. For a part of his term the family lived in Washington with him, rooming at Mrs. Spriggs's. But some of the time Mrs. Lincoln stayed at her father's in Kentucky. The letters between husband and wife during this period reveal the tender affection that united the couple and their deep devotion to their children. Writing from Washington in 1848, Lincoln found himself lonesome for his wife in Kentucky. To occupy his time he went shopping for plaid stockings to fit "Eddy's dear little feet." "All the house," he wrote Mary, "or rather, all with whom you were on decided good terms—send their love to you—The others say nothing." He was concerned with his "Molly's" health. "Are you entirely free from headache?" he asked. "That is good . . . I am afraid you will get so well, and fat, and young, as to be wanting to marry again."

She replied in kind, telling the family news, how little "Eddy" had recovered from a spell of sickness, and how the children had adopted a homeless kitten. She concluded: "Do not fear the children, have forgotten you, I was only jesting. Even E-eyes brighten at the mention of your name." Others letters at this period tell of a husband's anxiety to see his wife—provided she would "be a *good girl* in all things": when she came East—and of his worry about an accumulation of debts. Later Lincoln wrote impatiently that he had "expected to see you all sooner" and closed with "Kiss and love the dear rascals." These were the sort of letters that an understanding and adjusted couple would write.

When the term in Congress was over, Lincoln returned to Springfield, to the practice of law and the pursuit of politics. Mary was a help to her husband; she had influential family connections; she could guard against social blunders; she read books for Lincoln; she understood politics and was a good judge of character; she carried on the church responsibilities for the pair; she could entertain and charm visiting politicians. In short, she was the wife Lincoln needed.

III

How can one summarize twenty-two years of married life— the endless round of domestic duties, the cycle of birth and growth, the silent adjustments of man and wife? Springfield was home to the Lincolns. The house on Eighth Street was where their children grew up. Every foot, every inch of it had memories, suggestions of the compromises and truces, the shared joys and griefs, the whispered hopes and silent dreams that make up a marriage. Little Eddy died in his fourth year, but his place was filled by two more sons, the ubiquitous and exuberant Tad, with his slight stammer, and bright little Willie, who was to die in Washington in 1862. Everyone agreed that the Lincolns were devoted parents. Perhaps they were overindulgent, and perhaps they loved their children too much. But any mother who could bring up three of four children in an age of terrific infant mortality, when cholera epidemics swept the country, before the days of the most rudimentary sanitation or sewerage, must have been a competent one.

A lawyer's income is irregular and somewhat uncertain, and Mary Todd Lincoln had at times to manage the meager resources. She did her own and the boys' sewing and sometimes did all the cooking for the family. When he was home, Mr. Lincoln milked the cow, curried the horse, and chopped wood for the stove. There was no time to plant and grow flowers about the place; even the garden the Lincolns tried one year was too much of a burden.

Springfield store records tell a good deal about this family of Lincolns. The books of John Williams & Co., dry goods merchants, carry such items as "2½ yds. Muslin per Lady," "1 pair Boys Boots," "4½ yds. Velvet Ribbon @ .06¼," "½ lb Gun Powder Tea @ 1.25," "2 pair Heavy Drawers @ 1.25," and "36 yds Buff Linen @ .25"—all charged to the Lincoln account. At Corneau & Diller's drugstore their purchases included "Castor Oil," "Calomel," "Bottle Vermifuge," "1 paper Horse Powder," "2 bottles Extract Vanella," "Cough Candy," "Toilet Soap," and more than one "Bottle Allen's Restorative." Tradition has it that Mary Lincoln was a shopper difficult to please and that she frequently exchanged goods she had purchased.

The Lincolns had their share in the social life of Springfield. There were teas and dinners, even though Mrs. Lincoln sometimes had to make up for them by a scanty everyday table. The children as well as the grown-ups had their parties. On one special occasion the Lincolns issued over five hundred invitations to an entertainment, and more than three hundred persons actually attended the gathering at the Eighth Street residence. Letters of the period frequently mention "Mr. Lincoln & Cousin Mary" as being present at suppers, at political receptions, at charity socials.

Mary's sister has left a picture of the Lincolns at this time: "Mr. Lincoln enjoyed his home and he and Mary idolized their children. So far as I could see there was complete harmony and loving kindness between Mary and her husband, consideration for each other's wishes and a taste for the same books. They seemed congenial in all things."

IV

IT IS A MISTAKE, however, to think of this marriage as one of uninterrupted happiness and tranquillity. The Lincolns had sharply contrasting personalities, and there was friction, as in every home. Mary had difficulties with housemaids, icemen, storekeepers, and delivery boys, and her husband must have understood that her outbursts of temper were connected directly with the violent headaches of which she had complained for years. When there was trouble, Mary Lincoln's temper sometimes got the better of her, and she would become momentarily irresponsible. There were many pressures beating on this woman, and she was not adapted either by temperament or by training to make a successful adjustment. Lincoln's law practice kept him on the circuit nearly half of the year, leaving his wife with two or three small children anxiously worrying at Springfield. There is something pathetic in Mary Lincoln's confidence to a neighbor: "She always said that if her husband had stayed at home as he ought to that she could love him better . . ."

And when Lincoln was at home, there were disagreements that sometimes became tempestuous. Mrs. Lincoln could never get used to seeing her husband stretched out on the floor of the parlor reading; and Lincoln could never break himself of the habit of answering the doorbell in his shirtsleeves or of using his own spoon in the sugar bowl. He was a man of long silences and brooding melancholy; she wanted lively talk and gay company. There were disputes over the children and how they should be trained. And there was the constant problem of servants, who were, for the most part, idle and inefficient and utterly unable to get along with the temperamental Mrs. Lincoln. After one particularly bad wrangle with a new servant girl, Mary sighed: "Well, one thing is certain: If Mr. Lincoln should happen to die, his spirit will never find me living outside the boundaries of a slave state."

When the strain became too great, Mrs. Lincoln would, as Herndon put it, "get the devil in her" and fly up in uncontrollable anger. At such times Lincoln would first of all ignore her. Then, if she did not calm down, he would take one of the children and leave the house until her fury was spent. There are a number of stories about these rages of hers; Springfield gossips were to smack their lips over them for fifty years. One man recalled passing the Lincoln house one Sunday and seeing "a woman chasing a man with a table knife or butcher knife in her hand"; when they came to a group of Springfield worthies returning from church, Lincoln "turned suddenly around, caught his wife by the shoulder with one hand and with the other caught his wife at the heavy end, her hips, if you please, and quickly hustled her to the back door of his house and . . . pushed her in, at the same time . . . spanking her heavy end, saying . . . 'There, d—n it, now stay in the house and don't disgrace us before the eyes of the world.'"

Once, so the story goes, Mary "blazed away with her sharp and sarcastic tongue" at a man who called at the house on business. She called him "a dirty villain—a vile creature & the like." When he complained to Lincoln, that unchivalrous gentleman is supposed to have said; "*Friend* . . . , can't you endure this one wrong . . . for old friendship's sake while I have had to bear it without complaint and without a murmur for lo these last fifteen years?"

Not all the temper, rumor had it, was on one side. One day Springfield citizens were shocked to see Mrs. Lincoln ejected forcibly from the Lincoln house, her husband shouting: "You make the house intolerable, damn you, get out of it."

One cannot ignore or dismiss such incidents. At the same time, it ought to be remembered that such disturbances were not the usual thing in the Lincoln home. In every marriage there are tensions and stresses, and in many marriages the partners may lose their tempers. Furthermore, such stories are of the kind likely to be exaggerated and repeated with endless variations. Most such anecdotes come from unreliable sources and were recorded long after the event. That Mary Lincoln lost control of herself at times is admitted. Against this should be set the facts that she was a faithful and loving wife, that she was a capable, if indulgent, mother, that she managed a growing household with commendable economy, that she performed graciously her duties as wife of a leading politician and lawyer. If storms occasionally struck the Lincoln house with unusual violence, disaster was avoided by the spirit of tender love and deep understanding that united the couple around their home and children. James Gourley, who lived next door to the Lincolns for nineteen years, gave a pretty fair verdict: "Mrs & Mr Lincoln were good neighbors."

The history of Mary Lincoln in the White House is another story, too long and too painful to be related here. Subject to the pitiless searchlight of unfavorable publicity, engulfed in the tidal wave of hate engendered by the war, bruised by the terrific responsibilities of her position, and desolated by intolerable grief, first over the death of a dearly loved son and then over the assassination of a husband more than life to her, her mind gave way. In her last tragic years, in that ceaseless seeking for peace which sent her searching over two continents, finally to seal herself in a shuttered, candlelit room in Springfield, her mind must often have wandered back—to the days of her marriage, to the birth of her children, to home and husband. She counted over her hours of past happiness like a rosary. Endlessly she fingered the gold wedding ring inscribed: "Love is Eternal." And as her wretchedly aching brain relived the past, she could clearly remember two things: she was Mrs. Abraham Lincoln, and she had made her husband a home.

SEVEN

Refighting the Civil War

I

THERE MUST BE more historians of the Civil War than there were generals fighting in it, and of the two groups, the historians are the more belligerent. They assume positions as resolutely as ever did Ulysses S. Grant, and they refight campaigns with all the slashing bitterness of N. B. Forrest. Monthly, almost daily, there appear in the bookstores new biographies, tracts, treatises, and general histories, all designed to reveal — "definitively," in each case, according to the publishers — who won the war and why.

One brigade of these historians is enthusiastically pro-Lincoln. John G. Nicolay and John Hay, the President's official biographers, established this party line, and their disciples have remained entrenched behind it ever since. Writers like John Ropes, Carl Sandburg, Collin Ballard, and Frederick Maurice believe that Lincoln had an intuitive mastery of strategy. In the West, where he had a free hand, he singled out Grant and Sherman for top commands. In the East he was hamstrung by politicians and political generals. All these writers believe that the President was correct in thinking McClellan too slow, in believing that he failed to capitalize upon his early advantages in the Peninsula campaign, and in feeling that he pursued Lee too weakly after Antietam. In the last year of the war Lincoln exhibited an amazing understanding of the general strategic picture, and, when necessary, he even called Grant to account. According to T. Harry Williams, "Lincoln stands out as a great war president, probably the greatest in our history, and a great natural strategist, a better one than any of his generals. He . . . did more than Grant or any general to win the war for the Union."

Such claims are earnestly refuted by the pro-Grant school of Civil War historians. Admitting that the President, though ignorant of warfare, had basically "a true military instinct," and praising him for his support of his ablest generals, these writers feel that it was Grant who was the master strategist, the architect of victory. This theory derives from Grant himself, for in his *Memoirs* the old general recalled how Lincoln proposed a preposterous plan of strategy that had to be tactfully disregarded. J. C. F. Fuller is sure that Grant was the greatest commander produced by the war; "whilst Lee fought like a paladin, as a general-in-chief he was inferior to Grant." The five volumes of Kenneth P. Williams's *Lincoln Finds a General* support this contention. "Ulysses S. Grant remains unique after two world wars," Williams believes; "he is still in many ways the most profitable and the most inspiring of all generals to study. He was a soldier's soldier, a general's general."

Sharply opposed to both these views is the theory that McClellan was the great Northern general of the war. McClellan himself maintained this position, and it has received its most emphatic statement in the writings of J. G. Randall. McClellan, Professor Randall points out, "created an efficient army out of an unmilitary aggregation . . . Never did the Union army under McClellan suffer a major defeat." His plan for warfare on the Peninsula was sound, sensible, and successful until there came "the incredible order . . . from Washington to drop it all and leave the Peninsula." Radical politicians had mobilized against the successful general, and Lincoln had weakly capitulated. It was McClellan who "saved Washington and the Union cause at Antietam." In summary, Professor Randall argues: "In 1862 he had planned to operate against Richmond from the south as Grant did in 1864; there is reason to believe that he would have succeeded as well as Grant did, and far sooner."

So far as Southern generalship is concerned, most writers unite in praise of Robert E. Lee, though J. C. F. Fuller, Kenneth P. Williams, and T. Harry Williams have strong reservations. Douglas S. Freeman's monumental *R. E. Lee* seems, however, to have fortified the South-erner's reputation against such sniping. In *A Hundred Years of War* the English historian Cyril Falls agrees that Lee "represents one of the supreme examples in military annals of the combination of strategist, tactical genius, leader of the highest inspiration, and tech-nician in the arts of hastily fortifying defensive positions superbly chosen . . . He must stand as the supreme figure of this survey of a hundred years of war."

If Lee was superb, military historians must offer some explana-tion why the Confederacy failed in battle, and a number of writers have pointed to Jefferson Davis as the villain. From the contempo-rary Richmond editor E. A. Pollard through Frederick Maurice, writers have stressed that Davis meddled in military affairs, that he distrusted able leaders like Joseph E. Johnston, and that he retained incompetents like Braxton Bragg and Lucius B. Northrop in responsible positions. "His weaknesses," Frederick Maurice argues, "were due to his failure to insist that the interests of the Confeder-acy as a whole should take precedence of the interests of the indi-vidual States, to an excess of caution, and to a tendency to rely too much on his small military experience, which caused him to con-cern himself with minor details."

Such groupings give only the main outlines of the historio-graphical battle. Almost no Civil War general, however obscure, has lacked his apologist—and his assailant as well. Over such minor figures as Fitz John Porter and Braxton Bragg veritable historical battles have been fought, and in recent years even John Pope has found a defender. W. T. Sherman and Stonewall Jackson, George Thomas and Joseph E. Johnston—each, it is claimed, was the best general in the war.

II

TO RESCUE CIVIL WAR HISTORY from personal partisanship, to understand why the commanders behaved as they did, to relate the military events of the conflict to broader economic and social patterns in American life, one must look at warfare as a social institution. From the age of the cavemen to the day of the hydrogen bomb, men have warred, but the manner in which they have organized their forces, the weapons that they have used, and the objectives for which they have fought have varied enormously. In one period a war results in the extermination or enslavement of enemy populations; in another, the protection of civilian life and property except that which is directly required for the defeat of enemy troops. Each age has its own views about the nature of warfare. A commander's course of action depends not merely upon the resources at his disposal but upon the objectives that he believes to be professionally and morally defensible. One cannot understand the course of a war unless he first knows the theory of warfare behind the fighting.

But in the American Civil War, it could be contended, most Union and Confederate army officers had no theoretical ideas about warfare at all. The United States was not a militaristic nation, and it had no real military tradition. It had fought one war against an indifferent enemy in 1812 and another against an inferior one in 1846, but it had not profited by these experiences. "There was not," T. Harry Williams writes, "an officer in the first year of the [Civil] war who was capable of efficiently administering and fighting a large army." Prussian General von Moltke had some justification for thinking the American conflict not so much warfare as the "movement of armed mobs."

On both sides, of course, there were officers who had been trained at the United States Military Academy, but at West Point they had learned something of mathematics, engineering, and "moral philosophy," a little about tactics, and virtually nothing of strategy. The science of war, investigators reported in 1860, "is made subordinate to almost every branch of instruction at the academy, and even 'veterinary science' is made the rival in importance . . ." Once they left West Point, even those graduates who remained in the regular army generally exhibited little interest in their profession. "There is now, in the Army," an infantry-tactics instructor related in 1860, "no incentive to exertion and study beyond the personal satisfaction each officer must feel who has a consciousness of having done his duty. The careless and ignorant officer is promoted, in his turn, with as much certainty as the accomplished one."

Still, all during the three decades before the war there were a few teachers and some students at the Military Academy who seriously studied their profession. With the Napoleonic era still so close, it was natural that they should turn to France for instruction and examples. In 1848 the instructors at West Point formed a "Napoleon Club" for the discussion of the Emperor's campaigns; George B. McClellan, G. W. Smith. D. H. Maury, and probably Robert E. Lee were among the members. And, like any serious student of the Napoleonic wars, they turned to the writings of Baron Henri Jomini. Born in Switzerland, Jomini early attracted Napoleon's attention by his military writings, and he was given a high position in the French army, from which he could observe the Emperor's strategy. Although he left the French armies to join the Czar's forces in 1813, Jomini continued to study Napoleon's career for the rest of his life, and by his death in 1869 he had published twenty-seven volumes of military history, covering the wars of Frederick the Great, of the French Revolution, and of Napoleon. In 1838 Jomini summarized his military theory in his *Précis de l'art de la guerre.* With no real rival except the German theorist Clausewitz, who wrote in an obscure fashion in a difficult tongue,[1] Jomini for half a century dominated military thinking in both Europe and America.

In the early days of West Point, Jomini's own writings seem to have been used as textbooks of strategy, but when they proved too difficult, abridgments and translations were substituted. Robert E. Lee's class, for instance, read Gay de Vernon's work on the science of war, which frankly drew its ideas from Jomini, "whose work is considered as a masterpiece and as the highest authority." "Indeed,"

---

[1] The Library of Congress lists no American edition of any of Clausewitz's writings published before 1865. I have not discovered any Union or Confederate general who read Clausewitz.

declared Gay de Vernon, "no man should pretend to be capable of commanding any considerable body of troops unless he has studied and meditated upon the principles laid down by Jomini." Another adaptation of Jomini's principles was published in 1836 by Dennis Hart Mahan, who had studied in France for four years before returning to teach engineering at the Academy. Jomini's maxims concerning tactics were developed in William J. Hardee's *Rifle and Light Infantry Tactics* (1855), which was to serve as a textbook in both Union and Confederate armies, and his strategic principles were restated in Henry Wager Halleck's *Elements of Military Art and Science* (1846), which correctly made "no pretension . . . to originality in any part," for it was an almost literal translation of Jomini. In 1860 a new course in "the theory of strategy and grand tactics" was introduced at the Academy; the textbook was Jomini's *The Art of War.*

Every serious military student made Jomini's works his Bible. While Robert E. Lee was superintendent of West Point, he purchased a copy of the *Précis de l'art de la guerre.* George B. McClellan read Jomini with much care and thought he was "the ablest of military writers, and the first author in any age who gathered from the campaigns of the great generals the true principles of war, and expressed them in clear and intelligible language." After graduation from West Point, Ethan Allen Hitchcock studied Jomini. The strategic principles of P. G. T. Beauregard, declares his latest biographer, "were derived entirely from Jomini and Napoleon." By 1865, in addition to abridgments and paraphrases, there were at least six translations of Jomini's own books published in the United States. Even after he was made commander-in-chief of the Union armies, Halleck continued to edit Jomini's writings, and he viewed his translation of Jomini's *Life of Napoleon* (4 vols., 1864) as a practical contribution to the conduct of the Civil War. W. T. Sherman apparently felt the same, for in 1862 he directed his subordinates: "Should any officer, high or low, . . . be ignorant of his tactics, regulations, or even of the principles of the Art of War (Mahan and Jomini) it would be a lasting disgrace."

III

COLONEL J. D. HITTLE is correct, then, in saying "that many a Civil War general went into battle with a sword in one hand and Jomini's *Summary of the Art of War* in the other." In fact, the military history of the first two years of the war reads like little more than an exegesis of Jomini's theories. The views of the French writer were particularly acceptable to officers who were trying, often without adequate preparation, to put an army into shape for fighting. "Military science," said Jomini comfortingly, "rests upon principles which can never be safely violated . . . ," and he proceeded, in a series of maxims, to list these fundamental rules. It was no wonder that a second edition of Halleck's paraphrase of Jomini was required in 1861 or that the book "became a manual for most officers of the Army, and particularly for Volunteers."

Often Civil War commanders borrowed not merely the ideas but the very words of Jomini's maxims. When Jefferson Davis favored a strategy to which, as Frederick Maurice disparagingly remarks, "he gave the high-sounding title of 'offensive-defensive,'" he was consciously following Jomini's advice that "the defensive-offensive . . . may have strategical as well as tactical advantages. It combines the advantages of both systems; for one who awaits his adversary upon a prepared field, with all his own resources in hand, surrounded by all the advantages of being on his own ground, can hope with success to take the initiative, and is fully able to judge when and where to strike."

Perhaps the most famous of Jomini's maxims concerned the need for concentration of force upon the decisive point of a battle, which he termed "the guiding principle of strategy and tactics." Practically every general on both sides shared this belief. McClellan called concentration "the great principle which is the foundation of the art of war." "It is only by the concentration of our troops," wrote Lee in 1863, "that we can hope to win any decisive advantage." Beauregard analyzed the First Battle of Bull Run in words taken almost verbatim from Jomini: "The whole science of war may be briefly defined as the art of placing in the right position, at the right time, a mass of troops greater than your enemy can there oppose to you."

From tactics to superstrategy Jomini supplied the rules to both Union and Confederate commanders. Basically the French theorist pictured a tactical situation in which armies were drawn up in opposing lines of battle, one offensive, the other defensive. After an artillery barrage that blasted the enemy's lines to pieces, the commander on the offensive sent out his infantry, "undoubtedly the most important arm." Protected on either flank by cavalry, foot soldiers would make a bayonet charge and put their opponents to rout. For such an assault close-order drill was necessary, and Hardee's *Tactics*—and all the imitations of Hardee used in both armies—gave elaborate instructions on "Formation of a Regiment in order of Battle," "Principles of Shouldered Arms," how "to halt the company marching in line of battle, and to align it," and so on.

Believing that "the offensive is almost always advantageous," Jomini was opposed to earthworks and fortifications. "To bury an army in entrenchments, where it may be outflanked and surrounded, or forced in front even if secure from a flank attack, is manifest folly," he ruled; "and it is to be hoped that we shall never see another instance of it." At the outset Civil War commanders obeyed Jomini's maxim. Confederates, "scorning the shelter of fortifications as unworthy of gentlemen in arms, . . . were not disposed to construct them," and Northern commanders, too, opposed such defenses as cowardly. "We did not fortify our camps against an attack," Sherman wrote of the battle of Shiloh, "because we had no orders to do so, and because such a course would have made our raw men timid."

For the actual conduct of battle, Jomini diagrammed twelve possible plans of combat—"the simple parallel order," "the parallel order with a defensive or offensive crotchet," "the order reinforced upon one or both wings," "the convex order," "the order by echelon on the center," etc. All this sounds theoretical, but careful analysis of individual engagements of the Civil War reveals that commanders were actually drawing up their troops in accordance with

Jomini's idealized schemes. At Antietam, for instance, McClellan literally adapted Jomini's plan for "the attack on both wings." The commander's design, in his own words, "was to make the main attack upon the enemy's left—at least to create a diversion in favor of the main attack, with the hope of something more by assailing the enemy's right—and, as soon as one or both of the flank movements were fully successful, to attack their center with any reserve I might then have on hand." Despite Burnside's slowness to advance, the battle was fought according to the rule book, and it was no wonder that McClellan wrote complacently afterward: "Those in whose judgment I rely tell me that I fought the battle splendidly and that it was a masterpiece of art." McClellan was always an admirer of Jomini, but after the war he noted, rather plaintively: "Jomini's book helps but does not create a general."

"In a war of invasion," Jomini wrote, "the capital is, ordinarily, the objective point," and for four years American armies battled for the strategically valueless positions of Richmond and Washington. Although Jomini sometimes seemed to share Clausewitz's belief that the object of war is the destruction of the enemy's armies, on the whole he—and more particularly his American translators and editors—tended to think that the primary object of military operations was the occupation of enemy territory. General Fuller is doubtless quite correct by modern standards in thinking that the Confederacy should have kept Montgomery as its capital, strongly held Gulf and Atlantic railheads, and lured Union armies southward over constantly extending lines of communication, but Confederate leaders could no more disenthrall themselves from Jomini's theories than they could from a belief in slavery or state rights.

Jomini thought of war as an affair for professionals, not for the politicians or for the people. Although he had witnessed the great popular uprisings of the French Revolution, his prejudices were "in favor of the good old times when the French and English Guards courteously invited each other to fire first,—as at Fontenoy." For a people to rise up in arms would have "consequences . . . so terrible that, for the sake of humanity we ought to hope never to see it." Nor did he approve of ideological or propaganda warfare. "Although it be permitted us to believe that the support of political dogmas is at times an excellent auxiliary," he conceded, "it must not be forgotten that the Koran even would gain no more than a province at this day, for in order to effect this, cannon, shells, balls, gunpowder, and muskets are necessary."

Only against this background can one understand one of the strangest episodes of the Civil War, McClellan's "Harrison's Landing" letter to Lincoln of July 1862, in which the general told the President that the war must not be waged for "the subjugation of the peoples of any State" and protested against "confiscation of property, political executions of persons, territorial organization of States, or forcible abolition of slavery." Often treated by historians as an incredible aberration on McClellan's part, or as a political document designed to win him the next Democratic presidential nomination, the letter was, in fact, merely a statement of what McClellan thought to be Jomini's principles; he believed that war ought to be fought by soldiers on the battlefield.

IV

DURING MUCH OF THE WAR, then, Northern and Southern generals fought according to the same rules. All the moves and all the responses were laid out in the books. The war was rather like an elaborate quadrille. As more Southern commanders had attained a high rank at West Point and had remained in the army afterward, Confederate leaders on the whole could outsmart their former classmates from the Academy, who had studied from the same books, and, anticipating their actions, could bring about their defeat.

But while military men applied Jomini's formulas, technological changes were rapidly making his rules inapplicable. Jomini was writing of warfare in the Napoleonic era, not of a civil war in the mid-nineteenth century. The French writer thought of an infantryman armed with a muzzle-loading musket capable of being loaded perhaps twice a minute and having an effective range of one hundred yards. It was, as General Fuller writes, "a most inaccurate weapon, so inaccurate that the smoke-cloud it produced was of as great an assistance to the bayonet assault as the bullets fired."

American soldiers in the Civil War were equipped with rifles, which were not only more quickly loaded but also had an effective range of about eight hundred yards. The new weapon created "a totally new kind of infantry," and it made the textbooks of tactics obsolete. General Fuller has summarized some of the more revolutionary changes: As the last half-mile of an advance now had to be made under accurate enemy fire, frontal attacks became unprofitable, and, "generally speaking, nine assaults out of every ten failed." Gettysburg and Cold Harbor are two grim reminders of the power of the rifle. Consequently, the bayonet was seldom used. Surgeon-Major A.G. Hart declared that he had seen few bayonet wounds "except accidental ones . . . I think half a dozen would include all the wounds of this nature that I ever dressed." The heroic cavalry charge, with rearing horses and flashing sabers, also became obsolete. "Their own officers admit," wrote a disgusted English observer, "that the charges either of Cavalry or Infantry are purely imaginery [*sic*]; they may and have occasionally made a rush; but never get within 300 yards of one another; but normally wavered, halted, and fired irregularly and then one side or the other gets tired first [and] bolts, led by their officers . . ." Because of the added distance the rifle put between the two armies, infantry now often had time to entrench. The total result was to give a great advantage to the army that remained on the defensive. As Theodore Lyman wrote, "Put a man in a hole, and a good battery on a hill behind him, and he will beat off three times his number, even if he is not a very good soldier."

What the rifle did to Jomini's tactics, the railroad did to his strategy. Jomini's dictum that an army could move a maximum of twenty-five miles a day was now, of course, obsolete. The locomotive ground his maxims under its iron wheels. The introduction of the railroad meant also that the superiority of interior lines of communication, which Jomini so stressed and upon which the Confederates so securely relied, had to be modified. If interior lines were muddy roads and exterior ones iron rails, there was no question where the advantage lay.

The widespread introduction of labor-saving machinery also helped change the whole character of warfare. When one of McKay's sewing machines could produce shoes one hundred times as fast as they had formerly been made by hand, when a single McCormick reaper could replace six field hands, strategists no longer had to think in Jomini's terms of small professional armies fighting for a brief period of the year. The new technology made it possible to keep huge armies of citizen conscripts in the field almost indefinitely.

Because of these changes General Fuller is justified in writing "that the Civil War in America was not only one of the most remarkable ever fought, but one of the most important in the history of the evolution of war." Old theories of warfare had to be adapted to meet new technological facts.

On the tactical level, the ablest generals of both North and South speedily modified the rules they had learned at West Point. Lee was a brilliant tactical innovator. At Chancellorsville and at Antietam he disregarded Jomini's injunctions about concentration of force. After Gettysburg he realized that artillery was best employed as a defensive weapon. From the Mexican War he had acquired an accurate appreciation of the value of fortifications, and one of his first acts upon assuming command of the Army of Northern Virginia was to order the construction of earthworks. At first his men jeered at him as the "King of Spades," but they learned that one man in a trench was worth three in an assault. Grant, too, after his army was caught surprised, divided, and unprotected at Shiloh, had his men throw up works every time they halted. As the Union army wormed its way through the Wilderness, his soldier worked each night "with only bayonets, cups, two or three picks, and as many shovels to throw up a breastwork." The supreme example of the new tactics was the Atlanta campaign, where Joseph E. Johnston, who had doubted Jomini's soundness as early as 1860, opposed Sherman in a war of entrenchment and maneuver.

V

TECHNOLOGY COMPELLED BOTH SIDES to modify their tactics, but it was harder to revise basic strategic concepts. In the Union high command such generals as McClellan, who agreed with Jomini in predicting: "Woe to the general . . . who trusts in modern inventions, and neglects the principles of strategy . . . [which] will remain unchanged through all the improvements of the future," had to be set aside. Halleck, with his insistence upon concentration and his querulous attacks "against this *scatteration* system," had to be ignored. The new team of Lincoln, Grant, and Sherman was evolving a new kind of war.

The Confederate high command never succeeded in making such an adjustment. There was, for instance, no Confederate parallel to Grant's Vicksburg campaign, in which he deliberately, in violation of all the rules, cut himself off from his base of supply and lived on the country. Although the Southerners did use their limited railroad system, they could not rival the Union exploit of transporting about twenty thousand soldiers from Meade's army in Virginia to beleaguered Chattanooga in eight days. And the Confederates never exhibited that total disregard for Jomini's principle of concentration that Grant showed in 1864 when he ordered a "simultaneous movement all along the line," with Butler, Meade, Sigel, Averell, Crook, Sherman, and Banks all commencing independent, convergent assaults upon the enemy. There was no Jomini maxim equivalent to Lincoln's pithy summary of the order: "Those not skinning can hold a leg."

Each of these Union movements exhibited not merely audacity but also a new idea as to the meaning of warfare. Experimentally the Northern command was working toward a theory that approached Clausewitz's conception of total war. Sherman the innovator expressed it best: "My aim was, to whip the rebels, to humble their pride, to follow them to their inmost recesses, and make them fear and dread us. 'Fear is the beginning of wisdom.'"

Inevitably one asks why the Confederates, so brilliantly daring in tactical innovations, clung to Jomini's outmoded strategy. The answer in part must lie in the depletion of Southern resources. Davis could not afford to gamble. Lee understood the potential of railroads as well as Grant, but the South's straggly, worn-out lines, for which not one iron rail was rolled during the war, did not permit strategic daring.

In a way, too, the South was a prisoner of its early successes. Bull Run and the Seven Days, Fredericksburg and Chancellorsville had been won without drastic modifications of Jomini's rules, and the Confederate commanders lacked the pressure that failure gives to innovation. Because of these early successes there was little demand for frequent reshuffling of Confederate generals, and, in contrast with the North, there was a remarkable continuity in the Southern high command throughout the four years of war. The Confederacy offered little room for new faces and new ideas.

While the North searched out untried leaders and new theories, the South remained self-satisfied with the success of Davis and Lee. Temperamentally both were unreceptive to startlingly new ideas—as was the section from which they came. The Confederacy, as Clement Eaton has observed, was "truly a conservative revolt in that the South would not accept the nineteenth century." As other Southerners clung to outmoded ideas of Negro slavery and state rights, Lee and Davis retained to the end their faith in Jomini's maxims. A military martinet, stiff and unbending, Jefferson Davis was constitutionally incapable of experimenting. Lee, too, for all his marvelous tactical facility, was not fundamentally an innovator. At West Point he had the reputation of being a "Marble Model," the cadet who never got a demerit, the soldier who obeyed all the rules. As Freeman writes, "obedience to constituted authority had become so deeply implanted that it was almost a part of his religion." This was not the commander to introduce ideas of superstrategy, ideological conflict, or total war.

The victorious Northern team, on the other hand, knew few rules to forget and had fewer victories to overcome. With only a few months' comic-opera experience as a militia captain in the Black

Hawk War, Lincoln started out diffident and deferential to the military mind. But the professional experts failed him. The McClellans and Hallecks and Buells and Popes never seemed to have a general picture of the conflict; as Lincoln told Grant later, "They all wanted me to be the General." Overworked as he was, the President borrowed Halleck's *Elements of Military Art and Science* from the Library of Congress, read it and "a large number of strategical works," and tried to apply his good common sense to the broad military problem.

Grant, too, was not handicapped by early success. When he failed, he learned to try something else. It did not occur to him that his innovation might not be in Jomini's books, because he didn't read the books. Late in the conflict a young officer, doubtless intent upon promotion, flatteringly asked the general his opinion of Jomini and other writers upon the science of war. Grant replied that he had never read the French author. "The art of war," he said, "is simple enough. Find out where your enemy is. Get at him as soon as you can. Strike at him hard as you can, and keep moving on." Clausewitz could not have said more.

EIGHT

The Radicals and Lincoln

I

WHAT THE CIVIL WAR HISTORIAN NEEDS is a good villain. In Abraham Lincoln he has the ideal hero, but the purity of the President's character can best shine in contrast with the blackness of others' motives. As all good historians are frustrated dramatists, there have been many attempts to supply the necessary villainous relief. For a biographer like William H. Herndon there was no problem, for he pictured Jefferson Davis as Milton's Satan summoning up his Confederate hordes:

> *He call'd so loud, that all the hollow deep*
> *Of Hell resounded, Princes, Potentates, [etc.]…*
> *Awake, arise, or be for ever fall'n.*

But after Robert E. Lee and Stonewall Jackson were admitted to the national pantheon, and after the Lost Cause won in the history books what it never could on the battlefield, it was necessary to seek a new villain for the piece. The Republican laureates, John Hay and John G. Nicolay, found a substitute in the Northern Democratic party. It was under a Democratic President, they wrote, that the nation divided; it was Northern Copperheads who impeded the prosecution of the war; it was the Peace Democrats who nominated McClellan in 1864 in the great "Chicago surrender" to the forces of secession; it was the Democratic party that consistently opposed Lincoln's plans. Their theory was both dramatically satisfying and politically useful in the 1890's, but today it seems hopelessly dated. Contemporary Civil War historians, nearly all of whom are firm Democrats, are not inclined to view the triumph of the Republican party as an example of wonder-working Providence, and they have looked elsewhere for villains.

These recent writers, in fact, have given an ironical twist to the Nicolay-Hay story. Nearly every major contemporary writer on the Civil War period now finds the most serious opponents of Lincoln in the Radical wing of the Republican party. This "revisionist" interpretation runs somewhat as follows: Abraham Lincoln was an astute, farseeing statesman who would have won the war with expedition and ended it without bitterness. For the North he proposed malice toward none and charity for all; for the Negro, freedom, a gradual emancipation, possibly continuing till 1900; for the Southern whites, compensation for their slaves and amnesty for their rebellion in return for future loyalty. Preserving the Union and painlessly readmitting the reconstructed states, he would have bound up the nation's wounds, so that Americans could live in peace.

But these plans were frustrated, not so much by the Southerners, not even by the Democrats, but by a small yet articulate and potent group within the President's own party. These were the antislavery extremists, the "Jacobins," the Radicals. The true villains of the piece, they looked the part. There was malevolent and sharp-tongued old Thaddeus Stevens, whose uncertainly placed wig, protruding lower lip, and club foot made him "the perfect type of vindictive ugliness." Equally unlovely were the corrupt Ben Butler, with his "small, muddy and cruel eyes," perpetually crossed, and the constantly inebriated Zach Chandler, "that Zantippe in pants." The florid and arrogant Charles Sumner was of this group, as were pompous Salmon P. Chase, profane Benjamin F. Wade, and the "oleaginous" Edwin M. Stanton.

The abolitionist principles that these Radicals so piously announced were only a front for their real purposes. "Their main characteristics," according to J. G. Randall, "were antislavery zeal as a political instrument, moralizing unction, rebel-baiting intolerance and hunger for power." "They loved the Negro less for himself," T. Harry Williams adds, "than as an instrument with which they might fasten Republican political and economic control upon the South." For these unsavory Radicals were the advance agents of industrialism, which was about to take over the government of the United States and pervert it for selfish ends. Some of the Republicans openly admitted their economic objectives. John Sherman of Ohio said bluntly: ". . . those who elected Mr. Lincoln expect him . . . to secure to free labor its just right to the Territories of the United States; to protect . . . by wise revenue laws, the labor of our people; to secure the public lands to actual settlers . . . ; to develop the internal resources of the country by opening new means of communication between the Atlantic and the Pacific." Translated from politician's idiom, this meant that the Radicals intended to enact a high protective tariff that mothered monopoly, to pass a homestead law that invited speculators to loot the public domain, and to subsidize a transcontinental railroad that afforded infinite opportunities for jobbery.

Secession and the withdrawal of Southern Congressmen from Washington gave the Radicals a chance to enact their program, but an early end of the fighting might imperil their schemes. Ben Wade was, therefore, willing to see the war continued for thirty years, and Charles Sumner proclaimed: "I fear our victories more than our defeats. There must be more delay and more suffering . . .We are too victorious." When peace did come, it must be under terms that would never permit Southern and Western agrarians to challenge the Radical-fostered industrial supremacy. Abolition of slavery became not merely a humanitarian striving but a desperately needed political requirement, for only thus could a Radical like Wendell Phillips be sure that "the whole social system of the Gulf states is . . . taken to pieces; every bit of it." Emancipation alone was not enough, for the freedmen, loyal to the party that set them free, must have the ballot. ". . . I see no substantial protection for the freedmen except in the franchise," Sumner declared. "And here is the necessity for the universality of the suffrage: every vote is needed to counter-balance the rebels."

Toward those who would temporize, toward those who put Union before emancipation, toward those who merely wanted a speedy end to slaughter, these Radicals showed unsparing hostility. A general like McClellan was dangerous to them because he threatened to end the war without disturbing slavery. Wendell Phillips, Radical hatchet-man, went after his scalp: "I do not say McClellan is a traitor, but I say this, that if he had been a traitor from the crown of his head to the sole of his foot, he could not have served the South better than he has done since he was commander-in-chief; he could not have carried on the war in more exact deference to the politicians of that side of the union."

Equally suspect were Conservative civilian advisers to the President, such as William H. Seward, Edward Bates, Montgomery Blair, and Gideon Welles. Repeatedly the Radicals demanded a Cabinet reorganization, to oust the Conservatives and to put men of tested Radical mettle in their places. In December 1862 they organized a senatorial caucus and actually sent a delegation to the President demanding the removal of Seward. Only Lincoln's adroit political management averted a crisis and kept the Cabinet intact. But Radicals remained discontented. "We Republicans in the Northwest Wonder and are amazed," one of Lyman Trumbull's correspondents wrote, "to see pro Slavery Blair & Bates and envious ambitious Seward retained as chief advisers in the cabinet." "For God's sake," pleaded another, "let Congress pass a resolution asking the Prest to make Butler Secty. of War, Banks of the Navy, & Fessenden Secty of State, if he will not do it without."

Openly hostile to Lincoln's Conservative Cabinet aides, the Radicals were secretly antagonistic to the President himself. They said that they had no doubts about the President's honesty, but were gravely troubled about his lack of capacity and firmness. "The great weakness of the President is his everlasting playing Hawk and Buzzard," one of Greeley's friends complained. "Sometimes he is just and sometimes he is unjust. Sometimes he is wise and sometimes he is foolish. Sometimes he is earnest and sometimes he is joking.

Sometimes he is clear and sometimes he is muddy." By 1863 one New York Radical announced firmly: "The imbecility of the Government is so great, that its best friends can no longer use argument to defend its sheepishness—If Lincoln don't shew more determination, he will go out of office ten times more despised than the Traitor Buchanan. God save the country from politicians for warriors, and sheep for Presidents."

At every turn, then, these Radicals harassed the President. They meddled with military affairs and prolonged the war. They interfered with civilian administration and tried to wreck the Cabinet. They forced through brutal measures of confiscation that retarded the progress of pacification. They stressed the abolition issue at the cost of dividing Northern sentiment and prolonging Southern resistance. They opposed Lincoln's renomination in 1864, and even after he was officially selected by the Republican party as its standardbearer, they attempted to force his withdrawal and to run another, more Radical candidate in his stead. In 1865 they were ready to frustrate Lincoln's plans for speedy, peaceful reconstruction, just as they did, in fact, override those of his successor.

II

Such, then, are the new villains of the piece. Civil War historians agree upon so few matters that one hesitates to start another controversy by questioning this universally held interpretation, but there seem to be valid reasons for challenging the stereotype of Lincoln-versus-the-Radicals.

After all, these "Jacobins" have received rather unfair treatment from the historians. The men, rather than their principles, come in for condemnation. Radicals are characterized as ugly, vain, pompous, power-grabbing, dictatorial, inflexible, oleaginous, arrogant, and unctuous—all at the same time! Because Thaddeus Stevens is said to have cherished a mulatto mistress and Salmon P. Chase presidential aspirations, because Ben Butler had a cocked eye and Charles Sumner a passion for Latin quotations, all right-thinking readers are supposed to condemn Radicalism. In all justice it should be pointed out that physical attributes do not make a statesman. Abraham Lincoln never won a beauty contest. Is it not possible for a Senator to be vain, ambitious, and even unctuous — and still be perfectly correct in his views? The historian who indulges in name-calling makes his point by innuendo rather than by argument.

But if one grants that these Radicals were antislavery zealots, unlovely in body and in spirit, it is hard to see that they have entirely merited the abuse heaped upon them. The charge that they were spokesmen for the business interests of the North presupposes a degree of unity among these antislavery leaders that did not, in fact, exist. Most of them favored a high tariff, it is true — but so did most Conservative Republicans and many Northern Democrats, too. Other economic issues found the Radicals badly divided. It was Charles Sumner who introduced the first bill for Federal regulation of railroads ever proposed in Congress, and he was supported by Radical Horace Greeley, but other Radicals killed his measure in committee. Some Radicals spoke for the creditor classes in financial affairs, abhorred inflation, and demanded a return to a specie basis of currency, but Radicals Ben Wade, Thad Stevens, and Ben Butler all championed greenback inflation. Most Radicals — and, indeed, most Congressman — stood for the sanctity of private property, yet Stevens and Sumner proposed to create economic democracy in the South by dividing plantations among the freedmen — a proposal that other Radicals condemned as "a piece of political vengeance wreaked without the intervention of courts of justice, in defiance of the forms of law and to the ruin of the innocent and helpless."

If these Radical antislavery men were not united upon any positive social and economic program, they more nearly agreed about the things they opposed. But their dislike of slavery, of fumbling generalship, of presidential slowness, was shared by millions of Conservatives. It is true that Charles Sumner was bent on converting the war into an antislavery crusade, but so was his principal rival, the leader of the Massachusetts Conservative Republicans,

Charles Francis Adams, who declared in 1861: "We cannot afford to go over this ground more than once. The slave question must be settled this time once for all." Radicals were unhappy when Lincoln overruled General Frémont's proclamation freeing the slaves in his military district, but they were no more angry than was Orville H. Browning, one of the most Conservative of Illinois Republicans, who protested that the President's act was "damaging both to the administration and the cause" since Frémont's proclamation embodied "a true and important principle."

By 1862 nearly all Radicals opposed the retention of George B. McClellan in high command, but it is a serious error to equate suspicion of that slow-moving general with Radicalism. McClellan's long winter of inactivity, his unsuccessful campaign on the Peninsula, and his slowness to reinforce Pope at Second Bull Run left him with few congressional friends besides die-hard Democrats. At the same time that Radical George Perkins Marsh denied McClellan's "military capacity to command a platoon" and found "in his movement [not] so much evidence of stolidity, as of treachery," Conservative Edward Bates was complaining of the general's "criminal tardiness," "fatuous apathy," and "grotesque egotism." The famous Cabinet "round robin" of August 1862, protesting against McClellan's restoration to command, is incorrectly considered a "Radical plot" against the general. Secretary Chase's diary reveals that the document represented the opinion of all the Cabinet members except Seward and Blair. Conservative Attorney-General Bates willingly signed the "round robin," and Conservative Gideon Welles declined to do so only "on the grounds that it might seem unfriendly to the President," though he "agreed in opinion and was willing to express it, personally."

If Radical Congressmen were often critical of the President and his policies, it should be remembered that pretty nearly everybody else in Washington was, too. Some recent scholars seem to have forgotten the Democrats. Within the Republican party many opposed the President precisely because they thought he was a captive, if not a chief, of the Radicals. "Thousands of conservative republicans," wrote Dr. Caspar Wistar of Pennsylvania, "are sorely disappointed in Mr. Lincoln. He has abandoned himself . . . to the impracticable schemes of the radicalists . . . Mr Lincoln has given a death blow to our party by his insane course." Seward had correspondents who were ready to leave the Republican party because the President was "under the control of the Greeley's—Sumners and the band of 'fanatics' of the North."

Most of the opposition to Lincoln, whether from Radicals or Conservatives, arose simply because he seemed to be a failure as President. The famous senatorial caucus of December 1862, which sought to eliminate Seward from the administration, has often been treated as a Radical effort to take the reins from Lincoln's hands. In fact, however, that caucus was attended by all but two Republican members of the Senate, and Radicals and Conservatives joined in unanimously adopting two motions:

> *Resolved,* that in the judgment of the Republican members of the Senate, the public confidence in the present administration would be increased by a change in and partial reconstruction of the Cabinet.

> *Resolved,* that a committee be appointed to wait upon the President in behalf of senators here present and urge upon him changes in conduct and in the Cabinet which shall give the administration unity and vigor.

When the senatorial committee of seven confronted the President on December 17-18, it included such Radicals as Sumner and Wade, but its chairman and spokesman was Jacob Collamer, Conservative Republican from Vermont.

Nor can opposition to Lincoln's renomination in 1864 be correctly equated with Radicalism. It is true that many Radical antislavery men were discouraged and hopeless about Lincoln's prospects, but so was Conservative Thurlow Weed, who declared in August: "Mr. Lincoln's reelection is an impossibility." Lincoln himself believed that he would be defeated. And if some Radicals wanted to drop Lincoln from the ballot and substitute a more popular candidate, Thurlow Weed at one point had the same idea, because, he said, the people had "not had the worth of their Blood and Treasure" from Lincoln's administration.

III

ZEALOUS ANTISLAVERY MEN were often outspokenly critical of the President, but Lincoln was not in constant conflict with the Radical members of his own party. After all, the President's most consistent supporter in Congress was Radical Representative Owen Lovejoy. Some few of the Radicals—Wade and Henry Winter Davis, for instance—exhibited strong personal antagonism to the President, but with most of the group Lincoln managed to keep up a working political partnership. And with so inflexible a partisan as Charles Sumner, whom Gideon Welles considered "pre-eminently, the radical leader, and their ablest leader," the President developed bonds of personal and political friendship.

The relationship was difficult for both men, for there could scarcely have been two more different personalities. Handsome, Harvard-trained, and world-traveled, Sumner was the antithesis of the homely, self-educated President. With a decade's experience in the Senate, Sumner naturally regarded the untried Lincoln as "honest but inexperienced." A compulsive worker, proud of his prompt and thorough attention to his official duties, the Senator thought Lincoln's "habits of business . . . irregular" and felt that the President "did not see at once the just proportions of things, and allowed himself to be too much occupied by details." Sumner was proud of the purity of his diction, and he was pained when the President inelegantly said that the Confederates "turned tail and ran." Admitting that Lincoln occasionally wrote passages "unique in beauty and in sentiment," he nevertheless thought the President's style "failing often in correctness."

As Sumner had no sense of humor, he found conversation with Lincoln "a constant puzzle." The President tried to help; he took his feet down from the desk when Sumner entered the White

House office and he endeavored to be solemn. He even attempted to "initiate" Sumner into the mysteries of Petroleum V. Nasby, the humorous writer, and, laying aside official business for twenty minutes one day, "proceeded to read aloud, evidently enjoying it much." Sumner became restive and, "thinking there must be many at the door waiting to see the President on graver matters," solemnly thanked the President "for the lesson of the morning"—and left the White House as bewildered as he was unamused. "Mr. Sumner frequently—I might say almost always—failed to see the point of the quaint anecdotes or illustrations with which Lincoln was fond of elucidating his argument," Carl Schurz remembered. "Mr. Sumner not seldom quoted such Lincolnisms to me, and asked me with an air of innocent bewilderment, whether I could guess what the President could possibly have meant."

It seemed to the Senator that the President might well give his attention to the war instead of to witticisms. He found "no central inspiration or command" in the Northern military preparations. When defeat followed defeat, he complained: "It is hard—very hard—to witness this massacre of our fellow-citizens & this expenditure of our money—all for nothing." Foreign affairs, in which Sumner was particularly interested, seemed to be as badly managed as military operations. He believed that Secretary Seward still thought of provoking a European war in order to quiet the domestic one, and he protested that the Secretary "had subjected himself to ridicule in diplomatic circles at home and abroad; that he had uttered statements offensive to Congress and spoken of it repeatedly with disrespect in the presence of foreign ministers; that he had written offensive dispatches which the President could not have seen or assented to."

But most of all Sumner questioned the slowness of the Lincoln administration to act against slavery, "the origin and mainspring" of the rebellion. A doctrinaire idealist, Sumner was uncompromisingly committed to emancipation. It was a subject on which he could bear no disagreement; this "moral terrorist," as Schurz called him, viewed compromise on the slavery issue as evidence of turpitude. From the very beginning, Lincoln's pragmatic slowness vexed him. Again and again he lectured the President upon the necessity of immediately striking at slavery. He told Lincoln "plainly, that if he could not make up his mind to Emancipation, he must be ready to acknowledge the independence of the rebels." But Lincoln was dilatory, and the Senator acidly observed "that Mr. Lincoln resembles Louis XVI. more than any other ruler in history."

Sumner did not, therefore, favor the movement to renominate Lincoln in 1864, for he said that any member of the Massachusetts delegation to Congress was better qualified for the presidency. Perhaps he had one member in mind. Angrily hoping for "a president with brains," he thought that the Baltimore convention made "a great mistake" in renominating Lincoln, and as late as August 1864, he, along with Chase, Greeley, and others, hoped that the President would "see that we shall all be stronger and more united under another candidate" and withdraw from the race. When it became a clear-cut choice between Lincoln and McClellan, Sumner supported the former, but his campaign speeches were remarkable for giving the least possible attention to the merits of his party's choice. After the ballots were counted, Sumner rather ungraciously declared that the Republican victory was a "vote *against* McClellan rather than *for* Lincoln."

The last months of the President's life were vexed by open controversy with Sumner on the reconstruction of the South. The whole subject, the Senator warned him, "properly belong[ed] to Congress, according to the analogies of our govt, if not according to the terms of the Constitution." He agreed with Stanton in thinking that the approaching end of the war threatened "a crisis more trying than any before, with the chance of losing the fruits of our victory." When Lincoln proposed the speedy readmission of Louisiana under a government chosen by a fraction of the white voters in that state, Sumner went to the White House and told him firmly: "Mr. President, this bill ought not to pass, and it shall not pass." On the Senate floor he resorted to every obstructionist tactic within the realm of parliamentary law to prevent congressional approval of this "mere seven months' abortion, begotten by the bayonet, in criminal conjunction with the spirit of caste, and born before its time, rickety, unformed, unfinished, whose continued existence will be a burden, a reproach, and a wrong." Sumner killed the bill to readmit Louisiana, but he feared that the President's continued efforts to restore the Southern states augured "confusion and uncertainty in the future, with hot controversy. Alas! alas!"

I V

So FAR, THEN, the story of the President's relations with Sumner reinforces the view that the "Jacobins" were the most vehement and dangerous antagonists of the Lincoln administration. Real issues of principle between the two men did exist, and one must not minimize them; yet to picture the President and the Senator as embattled antagonists is not merely to do an essential disservice to both men but to misunderstand the nature of American politics. The notable thing is not that Lincoln and Sumner often quarreled, but that, in spite of their disagreements, they managed to work together in personal and political relations.

These two men, so radically different, came to respect and ultimately to like each other. Lincoln knew that the Senator was incorruptible, if often irritating; Sumner came to see that the President wanted "to do right & to save the country." Feeling a "profound pity" for the President in his thankless labors, Sumner tried, even when being critical of the administration, not to "enter into a personal controversy." "I have always been frank with the President; very frank," he said, "but what has passed between us I have never communicated in any way to the public."

Mutual respect became something a bit warmer chiefly through the agency of Mary Lincoln, who found the handsome bachelor Senator one of the most congenial men in Washington. Sumner and Mrs. Lincoln wrote each other notes in French; they went for carriage drives; they lent each other books; and she sent him bouquets from the White House conservatory. So often did Sumner receive White House invitations that on one occasion Lincoln felt obliged to write him:

Mrs. L. is embarrassed a little. She would be pleased to have your company again this evening, at the Opera, but she fears she may be taxing you. I have undertaken to clear up the little difficulty. If, for any reason, it will tax you, decline, without any hesitation; but it if will not, consider yourself already invited, and drop me a note.

When Sumner did not feel himself on public display, when he was not posturing from a pedestal, he could relax and become, as Mrs. Lincoln found, "the most agreeable & delightful of men." ". . . He was a constant visitor at the W[hite]. H[ouse]. both in office & drawing room," Mrs. Lincoln later recalled; "he appreciated my noble husband and I learned to converse with him, with more freedom & *confidence* than with any of my other friends." The President, too, found that the Senator had qualities of personal charm. Those who saw Sumner only as the "cold & haughty looking" abolitionist fanatic might find it hard to believe, but Mary Lincoln declared that her husband and the Senator used to talk and "laugh together like *two* school boys."

But had the men been personally antipathetic, political expediency would have required them to get along with each other. For a decade before 1861 Sumner had been an opposition Senator, and he was not disposed to break from his party in its day of victory. He found it pleasant to be part of the administration. When friends commented on the frequency with which he attended White House balls and levees, he replied: "This is the first administration in which I have ever felt disposed to visit *the house* and I consider it a *privilege*." A privilege it was, too, to become chairman of the potent Senate Committee on Foreign Relations and to be invited in for Cabinet meetings when a crisis like the *Trent* affair was under discussion. It was pleasant to be in a position where he could assist old political and personal friends with appointments, and Sumner was happy to think that such men as Motley, Palfrey, and Burlingame raised the level of the government service.

Even when he and the President disagreed, Sumner knew that he had direct access to the White House and could plead his case with Lincoln. Believing the President unjustifiably slow in moving against slavery, Sumner almost daily urged upon Lincoln "the most unflinching vigor, in the field & in council," and demanded "a positive policy on slavery." He thought that his talks were effective. *"The Presdt. tells me,"* he reported in December 1861 with great jubilation, "that the question between him & me is one of 4 weeks or at most 6 weeks, when we shall all be together." As long as he maintained a position of such influence Sumner was bound to "comprehend the wisdom of not breaking with the Chief of the Republic in this hour of fiery trial."

For Lincoln, too, expediency dictated that he continue on good terms with the ponderous and self-centered Massachusetts Senator. Count Gurowski was probably right in reporting that the President found Sumner "not very entertaining," but Lincoln rarely allowed the Senator's overbearing manner and his assumption of infallibility to provoke him. The President might have agreed with a shrewd Boston analysis that Sumner suffered from "prolonged & morbid juvenility," for he handled the stately Senator as a wise father does an unruly child. As far as possible, he controlled Sumner through praise, and he permitted him to believe that he was exercising a major force in the administration. "Don't I get along well with Sumner?" Lincoln once jokingly asked another Congressman; "he thinks he manages me." But when the Senator became impossible, the President found it best to ignore him. "I think I understand Mr. Sumner," he said; "and I think he would be all the more resolute in his persistence . . . if he supposed I were at all watching his course . . ."

Such tactics were necessary because, for all Sumner's homilies and importunities, the Senator was a useful ally. Sumner's voting record showed him to be a consistent supporter of most administration measures in Congress. His services were particularly valuable in the field of diplomacy, where, despite his grumbling against Seward, he served as an efficient chairman of the Senate Committee on Foreign Relations. His large and distinguished European correspondence sometimes enabled him to have a better idea of foreign opinion than did the Secretary of State. Through his letters to the Duke and Duchess of Argyll, the Senator could make his opinions heard even in the British Cabinet. Through Sumner the American government could keep in friendly touch with such supporters as Richard Cobden and John Bright. Lincoln gave to Sumner, for transmission to Bright, "a copy of a resolution drawn up by himself, . . . in his own autograph," intended to serve as a model that workingmen's conventions all over England could adopt in support of the Union cause.

In a similar way the Senator served as intermediary between the President and extreme abolitionist critics at home. As long as Sumner stayed with the administration, Wendell Phillips and Parker Pillsbury could have little success in alienating New England from Lincoln. In 1864, at just the time when antislavery extremists were planning to bolt the Republican party and nominate Frémont on an independent ticket, there was a rash of White House invitations, letters, and bouquets for Sumner. "I suppose," Francis Lieber cynically wrote the Senator, "all this civility to you in the White H. is to help getting L. right with the N. Engl. antislavery people."

Lincoln was determined that not even the reconstruction issue would divide him and Sumner. The President was seriously disappointed when Louisiana was not readmitted, and he became, as Sumner himself declared, "almost angry" at the Massachusetts Senator for his obduracy. "I can do nothing with Mr. Sumner in these matters," the President sadly declared. "While Mr. Sumner is very cordial to me, he is making his history in an issue with me on this very point." Washington gossip predicted an open rupture. "It is all up with Sumner," people said; "he has kicked the President's pet project down the Senate stairs."

But a historian must distinguish between a difference of opinion and a quarrel. Neither Lincoln nor Sumner desired to disrupt the Republican party. Neither man, at this stage, was unyieldingly committed to a specific program of reconstruction; hardening of the arguments had not yet set in. Feeling that their difference over reconstruction was "one of mere form and little else," the President anticipated "no essential contest between loyal men on this subject if they consider it reasonably." Cheerfully he agreed with Sumner on "the duty of harmony between Congress & the Executive." At the time of Lincoln's death, the two men were working toward an agreement, with Sumner perhaps yielding on the admission of Louisiana and the President promising fuller protection to Negroes in other ex-Confederate states.

To symbolize publicly his unwillingness to break with the Radical wing of his party over reconstruction, the President on March 5, 1865, sent a little note to Sumner:

> I should be pleased for you to accompany us tomorrow evening at ten o'clock, on a visit of half an hour to the Inaugeral-ball [sic]. I inclose a ticket. Our carriage will call for you at half past nine.

At half past ten on March 6 the band played "Hail to the Chief," and the crowd assembled in the Patent Office Building cleared a path so that the President, accompanied by the Speaker of the House, could reach the dais. Behind the Chief Executive came Mrs. Lincoln, in white silk and lace, escorted by that alleged foe of the administration Charles Sumner. "Abolitionism victorious," remarked one observer, "thus made its entry with the great force which had annihilated the enemy." Sumner more correctly evaluated the situation. The President, he said, "seemed to take this very conspicuous way of assuring the senators, representatives and people present that he still claimed me as a friend, and that a conscientious discharge of what I thought my duty, although directly opposed to what might be his favorite projects, would not sever or weaken our intercourse."

V

To picture Lincoln at swords' points with the Radical leaders of his own party, then, is an error. It is also a reflection of a naïve view of the nature of American politics. American Presidents are always criticized by members of their own parties. Politicians are constantly pointing with horror, invoking the just wrath of heaven, or threatening to take a walk. A historian ought not to be like Mr. Dooley's friend who mistook the annual beating of the carpets for the first guns of a revolution. Our major parties are awkward, agglomerate groups, each covering the entire range of political opinion. Naturally, important rivalries spring up within the parties, and the presidency becomes the center of a tug of war.

The Radical Republicans were only one of the many factions that pulled for control of the Lincoln administrations. Because they were noisy and conspicuous, their historical importance has been overrated. Beyond simply antislavery zeal, they held few ideas in common. There were pro-Lincoln Radicals and anti-Lincoln Radicals, just as there were pro-Lincoln Conservatives and anti-Lincoln Conservatives. Not until after Lincoln's death, during the Reconstruction era, can one speak of the Radicals as a unified political group.

President Lincoln realized the need to rally as many of these conflicting forces behind his administration as possible. He was a party man, and he tried to keep his party united. Far from breaking with the Radical Republicans, he tried to win their support. He worked with these men politically, and he got along with most of them personally. If antislavery zealots never gave Lincoln their full confidence, it was nevertheless the Radicals like Sumner, Stevens, and Chase who stayed behind his administration, while Conservatives like Reverdy Johnson, Seymour, and O. H. Browning were in the Democratic opposition.

Perhaps, then, it is time to discard the Malevolent Radical, along with the Copperhead Democrat and the Diabolical Southerner, as a stereotyped figure of evil. The historian must stop thinking of the Civil War in terms of hero-versus-villains and apply realistic political analysis to the great struggle. The drama of the Civil War is too serious to be treated as melodrama.

NINE

Abraham Lincoln and
the American Pragmatic Tradition

I

EVERYBODY ADMITS that Abraham Lincoln was a great statesman, but no two writers seem to agree upon the basis of his greatness. Some think he merits immortality as the spokesman of
Republican principles—whatever they may be—but others give
him most credit for being a kind of crypto-Democrat. In recent
years major historians have debated whether Lincoln was the
embodiment of the American conservative tradition or the per-
sonification of American liberalism.

Such arguments on the whole reveal more about their authors
than about Lincoln, and often they evidence more an inclination
to annex a major folk hero to some current cause than a desire to
accept the past upon its own terms. To most men of his own day
Lincoln seemed neither liberal nor conservative statesman; he was
simply a rather ineffectual President. It is hard to remember how
unsuccessful Lincoln's administration appeared to most of his contemporaries. He was, as J. G. Randall has pointed out in a brilliant
essay, "The Unpopular Mr. Lincoln," a man censured and distrusted by all parties. Friendly critics viewed him as honest, well
intentioned, but rather lacking in force; hostile ones, as weak, vacil-
lating, and opportunistic. They agreed in sensing an absence of
direction in Lincoln's administration, a seeming and puzzling lack
of policy.

As President, he appeared not to take hold. Before he was inaugurated, seven worried states of the Deep South seceded, but Lincoln did little to avert a crisis. He issued no public statements, announced no plans for peace, and apparently spent his time growing a set of whiskers. On his way to Washington in February 1861 his speeches bore the obviously erroneous refrain: ". . . There is nothing going wrong . . . There is nothing that really hurts anybody." After he was inaugurated, war broke out and four more states deserted Lincoln's government for the Confederacy. The President called for 75,000 nine-month volunteers to fight a war that was ultimately to enroll more than 2,000,000 soldiers on both sides and to cost $20,000,000,000. Northern newspapermen and politicians demanded a prompt advance against the Confederate armies, and under their pressure the President yielded and ordered the army "On to Richmond"—and on to Bull Run. Other disasters followed with monotonous regularity—the Peninsula campaign; Second Bull Run; Fredericksburg; Chancellorsville—and the few Federal victories were as costly as the defeats.

The President seemed unable to cope with the crisis. As an administrator, he appeared hopelessly incompetent. He was a born enemy of rules. His secretaries fought a constant and losing battle to systematize his schedule. For a long while he refused to put any restrictions upon the throngs of visitors, petitioners, and office-seekers who besieged his White House office. "They do not want much," he explained, "and they get very little . . . I know how I would feel in their place." Finally, under the pressure of urgent war business, the President was persuaded to limit these tiring visitors' hours, but even then he was constantly making exceptions for needy cases.

His Cabinet was of little help in organizing the war effort. For a while he held no regular Cabinet meetings at all. Then, when they were held, they seldom dealt with serious matters of policy. As a usual thing, Lincoln permitted each Cabinet officer to run his own department without control, guidance, or interference. When Secretary Chase presented proposed financial measures for his consideration, the President agreed without a question, saying: "You understand these things. I do not." But along with this aloofness,

Lincoln also had a fondness for what seemed to be random meddling with his administrators. Just when a Cabinet officer had
worked out some systematic plan for handling his department's
business, he would unexpectedly be greeted by petitioners bearing
brief but authoritative notes signed by the President: "Let this
woman have her son out of Old Capital Prison." "Attorney-General,
please make out and send me a pardon in this case." "Injustice has
probably been done in this case, Sec. of War please examine it."

As the war dragged on and defeat followed defeat, nearly every
segment of Northern opinion showed distrust of the unsuccessful
President. Copperheads, Radicals, War Democrats, Conservative
Republicans—all attacked Lincoln. Day after day indignant Senators and irate Representatives stalked into the White House, blus-
tering, threatening, cajoling, all demanding that the President take
a firm stand and do something—indeed, do almost anything—positive. "Let him," wrote Lincoln's disillusioned law partner, Herndon, "hang some Child or woman, if he has not Courage to hang a
man." "Does he suppose he can crush—squelch out this huge
rebellion by pop guns filled with rose water."

II

To such critics Lincoln amiably gave the often repeated
reply: "My policy is to have no policy." To men with plans, to men
with axes to grind or hatchets to use, the President's remark was
incomprehensible. Self-righteous Secretary Salmon P. Chase
snorted that it was an "idiotic notion." But Lincoln was not being
flippant or evasive; he was enunciating the basic premise of his
political philosophy and at the same time expressing the fundamental pragmatic element in the American political tradition.

The President's statement sounded simple, and if it had come
from another man, it might have revealed nothing more than simple-
mindedness. But when Lincoln said: "My policy is to have no policy,"
he was enunciating, either directly or by implication, a series of fundamental political principles.

(1) He was rejecting the doctrinaire approach to problems, declining to become attached to inflexible solutions or to ideological labels. Consistency meant little to Lincoln, and he refused to measure his associates by rigid tests of doctrinal purity. He was concerned with results. Long before the war, in 1844, he had energetically supported Henry Clay for President, believing that the Kentuckian, though himself a slaveholder, would not permit the further expansion of slavery. Simon-pure abolitionists took the opposing view—how could a real antislavery man vote for a slaveholder?—and they wasted their votes on the doctrinally pure but politically hopeless third-party candidate. Their vote helped elect James K. Polk and to bring on the Mexican War. To Lincoln the abolitionists' way of thinking seemed "wonderful." To their contention that "We are not to do *evil* that *good* may come," he countered with another, more apt biblical injunction: "By the *fruit* the tree is to be known."

A decade later, ironically enough, the situation was reversed, for conservative Whigs hesitated to oppose Stephen A. Douglas's Kansas-Nebraska scheme because they disliked to join the suspected abolitionists. "Good humoredly," Lincoln told his Whig friends that they were being "very silly," and he gave them some practical advice: "Stand with anybody that stands RIGHT. Stand with him while he is right and PART with him when he goes wrong. Stand WITH the abolitionist in restoring the Missouri Compromise and stand AGAINST him when he attempts to repeal the fugitive slave law."

So pragmatic an attitude was, of course, shocking to those Americans who lived by dogmas, by the hoary certainties of the past. No one could have exceeded Lincoln in his admiration for the founders of the Republic. "I have never had a feeling politically that did not spring from the sentiments embodied in the Declaration of Independence," he declared, and he spoke reverently of the "great authority" of the Revolutionary Fathers. But he warned his own age not to be bound by history. "The dogmas of the quiet past," he wrote, in an annual message to Congress, "are inadequate to the stormy present. The occasion is piled high with difficulty, and we must rise with the occasion. As our case is new, so we must think anew, and act anew. We must disenthrall ourselves, and then we shall save our country."

(2) Rejecting ideological labels, Lincoln tried to face political reality as it was, not as he would have it become. No man more carefully distinguished between "is" and "ought to be." On slavery, for example, Lincoln's personal views had long been a matter of public record. "If slavery is not wrong," he said simply, "nothing is wrong." But the President of the United States could not act as Abraham Lincoln wished. He was President not of the antislavery forces but of a disunited and divided people, and he must serve the general welfare. "I am naturally antislavery," the President declared. "And yet I have never understood that the Presidency conferred upon me an unrestricted right to act officially upon this judgment and feeling."

As a man he wished to eliminate slavery everywhere, but as President it became his official and painful duty to rebuke his subordinates who took extralegal steps to uproot the peculiar institution. When Generals John Charles Frémont and David Hunter issued edicts liberating the slaves in their military commands, Lincoln promptly overruled both commanders. Their hasty action would have cost the Union the support of the loyal slaveholders of Kentucky, and if Kentucky seceded, Missouri and Maryland might well follow. "These all against us," Lincoln explained, "and the job on our hands is too large for us. We would as well consent to separation at once, including the surrender of this capitol."

While Radical antislavery men grumbled about Lincoln's subservience to "negrophobic" counsels, the President was realistically warning his Southern friends that the war meant death for slavery. As Federal troops advanced into the South, flocks of Negroes left the plantations and fled to freedom. Whenever a raiding party returned from Virginia or Tennessee, it had behind it "an outlandish tatterdemalion parade of refugees, men and women and helpless children, people jubilant and bewildered and wholly defenseless, their eyes on the north star." It was not possible, the President advised their owners, to reduce these people again to slavery; there was no law that could remove the idea of freedom from the heart of a Negro. Earnestly Lincoln advised the border states to move toward gradual, compensated emancipation while there was still time.

Equally realistic was Lincoln's advice to the Negroes themselves. The President himself was color-blind; he shared neither the antislavery man's idealization of the Negro as God's image in ebony nor the slaveholder's view of the Negro as an inferior race. He had warm friends and countless admirers among the Negro people, and he thought of the black man first of all as a man. But again he separated his personal feelings from what he regarded as his official duty when he summoned a group of Northern free Negro leaders to the White House in August 1862. Plainly and painfully he told them the facts of life: "You and we are different races. We have between us a broader difference than exists between almost any other two races." Right or wrong, he continued, the difference meant that the Negro was unassimilable in American society. Freedom would not solve their problems. ". . . Even when you cease to be slaves, you are yet far removed from being placed on an equality with the white race. You are cut off from many of the advantages which the other race enjoy." If the Negroes wanted to avoid a future of menial subjection, they should think of colonizing, under United States protection, say in Haiti or in Central America. "It is better for us both," the President concluded, "to be separated." Such advice seemed inhuman to the idealists of the time, and it is unpalatable to the present-day liberal as well; yet clearly Lincoln had correctly analyzed the current state of American popular sentiment.

(3) Refusing to force reality to fit a formula, Lincoln insisted that every problem was unique, that issues could only be decided one at a time, that conflicts need be resolved only when they actually arose. Again and again he told anecdotes to illustrate his view. "The pilots on our Western rivers steer from *point to point* as they call it—setting the course of the boat no farther than they can see," he said, "and that is all I propose to myself . . ." He was not, he told a questioner, going "to cross 'Big Muddy' until he reached it."

War-torn and politics-ridden Missouri presented to President Lincoln a never-ending source of problems. Radicals and Conservative Republicans fought the secessionists, each other, and also the Federal military commanders in that state with about equal ferocity. All factions kept sending deputations to Washington, calling upon Lincoln to take a firm stand and commit himself to a clear-cut solution. The temptation must have been almost irresistible to take sides, to apply some simple formula to the Missouri problem in order to end the strife. Lincoln rejected the temptation. The Governor of Missouri demanded that the President recognize his right to appoint the commanding officers of the state militia; his political opponents urged that, as the militia was now in the Federal service, the appointments must be made by Washington. Quietly Lincoln bypassed the issue. He permitted the Missouri Governor to commission the officers first—and then he recommissioned them himself. "After a good deal of reflection," he explained to the Governor, "I concluded that it was better to make a rule for the practical matter in hand . . . than to decide a general question, . . . which, while it might embrace the practical question mentioned, might also be the nest in which forty other troublesome questions would be hatched. I would rather meet them *as* they come, than *before* they come, trusting that some of them may not come at all."

(4) The ability to face reality means, of course, a willingness to change with events. Lincoln willingly admitted that his opinions and his actions were shaped by forces beyond his control. His shifting position on emancipation clearly illustrates his flexibility. At first Lincoln and his administration were committed to the Crittenden Resolution, declaring that the purpose of the war was simply to restore the Union without disturbing slavery at all. Then the pressures for emancipation began mounting. By 1862 American diplomats warned that only a firm antislavery stand would check the pro-Confederate sympathies of France and England. Northern governors bluntly told the President that their antislavery young men were unwilling to enlist in an army still legally bound to preserve the hated institution. Military leaders like General Grant demanded

more men and pointed to the large numbers of Negroes who would willingly serve for their freedom.

As events moved, so moved the President. He was not going to act blindly, he assured a group of antislavery churchmen; there was certainly no point in issuing proclamations that "must necessarily be inoperative, like the Pope's bull against the comet." But he did act when ends and means were fitted, and the Emancipation Proclamation was a masterpiece of practical political sagacity. Lincoln rightly regarded the Proclamation as his chief claim to historical fame, but he was always careful to insist that it was a product of circumstances. He had responded to the changing times. In 1864 he wrote to an admirer: "I claim not to have controlled events, but confess plainly that events have controlled me."

(5) As a pragmatic politician, Lincoln was careful not to make irredeemable pledges against the future. Characteristically, he approached the difficult problems of reconstruction with an open mind and an absence of commitment. When Federal troops overran Louisiana and Arkansas, some sort of civil government had to be re-established, and the President, as commander-in-chief, had to act. He offered a lenient program of amnesty and reconstruction, under which the states would be restored to the Union if only 10 percent of the 1860 voting population assented. He did not attempt to set up loyalty tests that would disqualify former Confederates from participating in the elections. "On principle I dislike an oath which requires a man to swear he *has* not done wrong," he told Secretary Stanton. "It rejects the Christian principle of forgiveness on terms of repentance. I think it is enough if the man does no wrong *hereafter.*"

Lincoln's hopes for generous amnesty and quick restoration in the South have often been distorted by historians, who speak of "Lincoln's plan of reconstruction" as though the President had a blueprint for peace. It is true that later, in the unskillful hands of Andrew Johnson, Lincoln's suggestions were converted into dogmas, but it is important to remember that while Lincoln was alive his views on reconstruction were constantly changing. A shrewd observer like James G. Blaine felt "that Mr. Lincoln had no fixed plan for the reconstruction of the States."

The President did not take his own "ten per cent plan" too seriously as a program for action. To the military officials who supervised the Southern elections, he gave the pragmatic advice: "Follow forms of law as far as convenient, but at all events get the expression of the largest number of the people possible." The whole condition of the conquered South he thought "so new and unprecedented, . . . that no exclusive and inflexible plan can safely be prescribed as to details and colatterals [sic]." He himself, therefore, had one reconstruction program for Louisiana, another for Virginia, and yet another for Tennessee.

Lincoln repeatedly refused to commit himself to any theoretical position about the nature of reconstruction. The whole question of whether the seceded states were legally in or out of the Union he dismissed as "a merely pernicious abstraction." When extreme antislavery men urged that the Negro be given the vote, he did not, as did Andrew Johnson later, reply with a reminder that the Constitution left suffrage in the hands of the states. Doubtless Lincoln realized that the whole issue of reconstruction was by its nature extraconstitutional, that that venerable document no more contemplated the appointment of military governors for Southern states than it did the enfranchisement of the Southern Negroes by Federal enactment. As the case was unprecedented, so that action had to be unprecedented, without ritualistic invocation of constitutional sanctions. Very practically, Lincoln tried to solve the issue by writing to Southern leaders and urging that the ballot be given to some, at least, of the more intelligent freedmen, especially those who had served in the Union army.

Throughout all the discussion of reconstruction, Lincoln showed no pride of authorship. As he had been obliged to take some action in a conquered area like Louisiana, he explained, he had issued a proclamation outlining "*a* plan of reconstruction," but it was "not the only plan which might possibly be acceptable." The alternative, congressional proposals for reconstruction, embodied in the Wade-Davis bill of 1864, he pocket-vetoed—because he was "unprepared to be inflexibly committed to any single plan of reconstruction" and because he had not sufficient time to study so important a measure in the ten days after the adjournment of Congress. When he did examine it, he took the unprecedented step of recording his opinion of the Radical measure. It was not exactly what he himself preferred, he explained, but, he said, "I am fully satisfied with the system of restoration contained in the Bill, as one very proper plan for the loyal people of any State choosing to adopt it."

In the last public speech of his life, Lincoln once again turned to the difficulties of peace and urged bold and pragmatic facing of issues as they arose. Any "exclusive, and inflexible plan," he kept insisting, "would surely become a new entanglement." And he himself offered a practical example of what he meant by freedom from *a priori* commitments. His word was out to the government recently organized in Louisiana and now seeking congressional approval, and on the whole he believed that recognition of this government would be the surest way to secure peace in that state. But he was not blindly bound by his own words. ". . . As bad promises are better broken than kept, I shall treat this as a bad promise, and break it, whenever I shall be convinced that keeping it is adverse to the public interest."

III

ABSOLUTISTS THOUGHT that Lincoln's "no policy" theory was nothing but untrustworthiness, indecisiveness, and opportunism, and it is clear that pragmatism, misapplied, can be a polysyllabic synonym for drift. In Lincoln's case it meant something very different; it was an expression of his tragic realization of the limitations on human activity.

As a statesman, he was leader in a democratic society, and he firmly believed that such a free government represented "the last, best hope of earth." He knew that the successful democratic leader must not be too far ahead of his following. "Public opinion in this country," he had said before his election, "is everything." He did not have a naïve confidence that identified the popular voice with God's; he knew that the popular will was slow, blundering, and often mistaken. But no one could deceive all the people all the time, and, rejecting the flashy notion of authoritarian leadership with its claim to superior wisdom, Lincoln felt "a patient confidence in the ultimate justice of the people." In a free society one had to believe in the soundness of their final judgment. "Is there," Lincoln asked in his first inaugural, "any better, or equal hope, in the world? In our present differences, is either party without faith of being in the right? If the Almighty Ruler of nations, with his eternal truth and justice, be on your side of the North, or on yours of the South, that truth, and that justice, will surely prevail, by the judgment of this great tribunal, the American people."

Such a trust in the people could easily deteriorate into cosmic optimism, into Pollyanna's philosophy of history. But Lincoln did not mean it so, and his reference to "the Almighty Ruler" in connection with the popular will is significant. For, just as the President of a democratic country could only act within the limitations of a free society, so all men were restrained by forces and patterns larger than themselves. Back in Illinois Lincoln had often quoted fatalistically:

> *There's a divinity that shapes our ends,*
> *Rough-hew them how we will.*

As wartime President, he had greater reason to learn that man's plans are not always God's plans, that, in the haunting words of the second inaugural, "The Almighty has His own purposes."

In his own distinctively American way, then, Abraham Lincoln possessed what John Keats called the "quality [that] went to form a Man of Achievement," that quality "which Shakespeare possessed so enormously— . . . *Negative Capability*, that is when a man is capable of being in uncertainties, Mysteries, doubts, without any irritable reaching after fact and reason. . . ." Lincoln knew that there were limits to rational human activity, and that there was no virtue in irritably seeking to perform the impossible. As President, he could only do his best to handle problems as they arose and have a patient trust that popular support for his solutions would be forthcoming. But the ultimate decision was beyond his, or any man's, control. "Now, at the end of three years struggle," he said, "the nation's condition is not what either party, or any man, devised, or expected. God alone can claim it."

TEN

A Whig in the White House

THE PRESIDENCY of Abraham Lincoln poses a peculiar paradox to students of the American government. The most careful historian of the Civil War period, J. G. Randall, concluded that Lincoln extended the President's "sphere of activity throughout the whole government—civil and military, state and Federal, legislative and judicial as well as executive." A distinguished political scientist, W. E. Binkley, agreed that Lincoln unquestionably set "the high-water mark of the exercise of executive power in the United States." On the other hand, Edward S. Corwin, who made a lifelong study of the American presidency, noted that Lincoln, "a spoilsman" with no conception of the requirements of sound administration, failed to exert much influence over Congress and permitted the Civil War to be fought "by a kind diarchy," with each end of Pennsylvania Avenue carrying on its own campaign against the Confederates. Recognizing that Lincoln "added a new dimension to the Presidency in the presence of national emergency," Professor Corwin concluded that his incumbency was "in certain other respects a calamity for the office." The paradox has been most neatly posed in an able book, *The American Presidency*, by Clinton Rossiter, who asserted on one page that "Lincoln pushed the powers of the Presidency to a new plateau high above any conception of executive authority hitherto imagined in this country," but added on the next that "Lincoln . . . left the Presidency temporarily enfeebled."

I

FOR THE VIEW that Lincoln dramatically extended the range of executive power there is certainly abundant evidence. In 1861 when the Confederates fired upon Fort Sumter he acted with such vigorous promptness that his critics cried out against his "dictatorship." Without consulting Congress, he decided that a state of war existed, summoned the militia to defeat this combination "too powerful to be suppressed by the ordinary course of judicial proceedings," and enlarged the size of the regular United States army. Without congressional appropriation or approval he entrusted two million dollars of government funds to his private agents in New York in order to pay for "military and naval measures necessary for the defense and support of the government." Directing General Winfield Scott "to suspend the writ of Habeas Corpus for the public safety," he authorized the arbitrary arrest of suspected secessionists and other enemies of the government.

As the war progressed, Lincoln further extended his executive powers, even in the loyal states of the Union. "[B]y degrees," as he explained in 1863, he had come to feel that "strong measures" were "indispensable to the public Safety." Civil rights throughout the North were drastically curbed. Both Secretary of State William H. Seward, who was in charge of the arbitrary arrests made during 1861, and Secretary of War Edwin M. Stanton, who took control in the following year, exercised power "almost as free from restraint as a dictator or a sultan." It required but a line from the President to close down a censorious newspaper, to banish a Democratic politician, or to arrest suspected members of a state legislature.

Over the Union armed forces, too, Lincoln exercised unprecedented authority. Presidential order, not congressional enactment, instituted in 1862 the first national program of conscription in United States history. Disregarding the explicit constitutional provision that Congress should "make Rules for the Government and Regulation of the land and naval Forces," Lincoln authorized Professor Francis Lieber to draw up and General Henry W. Halleck to proclaim General Orders No. 100, spelling out the legal rules for the conduct of the war.

Lincoln took quite literally the constitutional provision that "the President shall be Commander in Chief of the Army and Navy of the United States." He not merely appointed and removed generals; he attempted to plan their campaigns. At his insistence General Irvin McDowell advanced to First Bull Run and to defeat in July 1861. Lincoln's unsolicited strategic advice drove General George B. McClellan, McDowell's successor, into hiding at the house of a friend so as to escape "browsing presidents." During the winter of 1861 when McClellan, ill with typhoid, did not advance, Lincoln issued his unprecedented President's General War Order No. 1, taking personal direction of five Union armies and two naval flotillas and ordering them simultaneously to advance on February 22. The fact that General McClellan, upon recovering, persuaded Lincoln to abandon his plan did not mean the end of presidential warmaking. In fact, even at the end of the war, after Lincoln had named U. S. Grant general-in-chief, the President continued to have a personal hand in shaping Union strategy. Lincoln himself bluntly declared that should he think any plan of campaign ill-advised, he "would scarcely allow the attempt to be made, if the general in command should desire to make it."

To an even greater extent Lincoln asserted his presidential powers over the rebellious South. His Emancipation Proclamation, which Charles A. Beard called "the most stupendous act of sequestration in the history of Anglo-Saxon jurisprudence," was a presidential act, performed without authorization from Congress— performed, indeed, when the President thought Congress had no power to authorize it. Lincoln's December 1863 proclamation of amnesty and pardon marked another major expansion of presidential powers. Without the approval of Congress he established provisional courts in conquered Southern states and gave them "the unlimited power of determining every question that could be the subject of judicial decision." In naming military governors for the states of Louisiana, Arkansas, and Tennessee, the President, again without congressional authorization, created offices unknown to the American Constitution. In establishing new and securely loyal administrations in these ex-Confederate states, the military governors were not obliged to observe normal constitutional procedures.

Lincoln's record, then, abundantly justifies the conclusion of George Fort Milton that no other President in American history has "found so many new sources of executive power, nor so expanded and perfected those others already had used."

II

BUT THERE IS ANOTHER ASPECT of the Lincoln administration. Less than any other major American President did Lincoln control or even influence the Congress. Noting that many of the Civil War congressmen were his seniors and humbly declaring "that many of you have more experience than I, in the conduct of public affairs," Lincoln bowed not merely to the will but to the caprice of the legislators. In making appointments, he regularly deferred to the Republican delegation from each state. He acquiesced in the Senate's right to veto appointments by refusing to resubmit any nomination that the Senate had rejected. Even upon a matter so clearly within presidential prerogative as extending recognition to Haiti and Liberia, Lincoln declined to act until Congress assented, because, he declared, he was "Unwilling . . . to inaugurate a novel policy . . . without the approbation of Congress."

The President had remarkably little connection with the legislation passed during the Civil War. He proposed few specific laws to Congress; his bill for compensated emancipation is notably exceptional. He exerted little influence in securing the adoption of bills that were introduced. In some of the most significant legislation enacted during his administration Lincoln showed little interest. The laws providing for the construction of a Pacific railroad, for the creation of the Department of Agriculture, for the importation of "contract laborers" from Europe, for the tariff protection of American manufacturers, and for the establishment of land-grant colleges had little connection with Lincoln aside from his formal approval of them. That approval was usually granted without hesitation. Less than any other important American President did Lincoln use his veto power. He vetoed only two measures outright, an unimportant bill concerning bank notes in the District of Columbia and an act dealing with army medical officers that carelessly duplicated another he had already signed. One of his two pocket vetoes was equally trivial. The other, his highly significant refusal to sign the Wade-Davis Bill, indicated that the President thought that reconstruction was an executive, not a legislative, responsibility. Within the area of what he considered legitimate congressional power Lincoln was careful never to interfere.

Lincoln was also ineffectual in controlling the executive departments of the government. He and his Cabinet never formed a unified administration. During his first months as President, Lincoln did not schedule regular Cabinet meetings at all. When he later did so, at the request of the Cabinet members themselves, he rarely discussed major policy decisions with his constitutional advisers. Sometimes the President himself was not present at these meetings, and soon the department heads became lax in attendance. The Secretary of State preferred to meet with the President privately—to regale him, enemies said, with vulgar stories; the Secretary of War declined to discuss his plans in Cabinet meetings because he thought, with some justice, that his colleagues could not be trusted with military secrets; Salmon P. Chase, the Secretary of the Treasury, refused to waste his time attending sessions of this "so-called Cabinet." "We . . . are called members of the Cabinet," Chase indignantly protested, "but are in reality only separate heads of departments, meeting now and then for talk on whatever happens to come uppermost, not for grave consultation on matters concerning the salvation of the country."

To most of his departmental chiefs Lincoln gave a completely free hand. His Attorney General, Postmaster General, Secretary of the Interior, and Secretary of the Navy conducted their departmental affairs virtually without oversight or interference from the President. Even over a critical area like the Treasury Department Lincoln exerted little control. Though some of the most important financial legislation in American history was adopted during the Civil War years, Lincoln had little interest in floating bond issues, creating an internal revenue system, inaugurating the first income tax, or establishing a national banking system. Repeatedly Chase tried to bring such weighty issues to the President's attention, but Lincoln brushed him aside, saying "You understand these matters; I do not."

Even in the conduct of foreign relations the President himself played a minor role. It is a charming fancy to think of Lincoln as a "diplomat in carpet slippers," applying homely common sense and frontier wisdom to the preservation of international peace. In fact, however, after curbing Seward's belligerent tendencies early in 1861, the President willingly left diplomacy to his able Secretary of State. In Lincoln's *Collected Works* there is notably little about foreign affairs, aside from routine diplomatic communications, which were of course written by Seward, extending congratulations to Alexander II of Russia upon the birth of a son named "Pierre to Madame the Grand Duchess Alexandra Petrovna, Spouse of Your Imperial Majestys well beloved brother His Imperial Highness Monseigneur the Grand Duke Nicholas Nicolaewitch" or offering condolences upon the demise of "His Royal Hig[h]ness the Hereditary Prince Frederick Ferdinand, of Denmark."

Even over the War Department, in which Lincoln took such a direct, personal interest, the President did not exercise unrestricted authority. Secretary Stanton, who resented Lincoln's meddling in his department, ran his affairs for the most part quite independently of executive control and often in close cooperation with the anti-Lincoln Congressional Committee on the Conduct of the War. Lincoln could, of course, have removed Stanton or any other recalcitrant subordinate, but, having put up with Simon Cameron in the War Department for nearly a year, the President was reluctant to lose a secretary who might be prickly and independent-minded but who was also honest and efficient. To an impatient friend who felt

Stanton had treated him unjustly, Lincoln explained his problem succinctly: "Of course I can overrule his decision if I will, but I cannot well administer the War Department independent of the Secretary of War." Indeed, instead of Lincoln's running his own War Department, it sometimes seemed that Stanton exercised a veto power upon the President. There was rueful humor in Lincoln's offhand refusal in 1862 to discuss military matters in a public speech: "The Secretary of War, you know, holds a pretty tight rein on the Press, so that they shall not tell more than they ought to, and I'm afraid that if I blab too much he might draw a tight rein on me."

Thus the same President who so drastically expanded the scope of his office by the assertion of his war powers under the Constitution was an executive who had singularly little impact either upon Congress or upon his own administrative aides. Just after his triumphant reelection in 1864, Lincoln remarked, with as much insight as wit, that he hoped he could exercise some influence with the incoming administration.

III

I<small>T IS NOT EASY</small> to reconcile these conflicting aspects of Lincoln's presidency. The common, and kind, explanation is that the wartime President, being a very busy man, had to concentrate upon the more essential aspects of his job and to slight the others. This argument would be more convincing if Lincoln had not devoted a quite extraordinary amount of his time to really trivial matters. He found it possible, for instance, to write an endorsement of his chiropodist on the same day he issued the Emancipation Proclamation. Nor does it solve the problem to say, with Professor Corwin, that Lincoln had a "temperamental indifference to problems of administration." In certain areas such as the discovery and testing of new arms and explosives, the President exhibited a keen interest in the most routine administrative details.

Perhaps an analysis of what Lincoln himself thought about the presidency may help resolve this paradox of a Chief Executive who simultaneously expanded and abdicated his powers. For more than a quarter of a century before his first election Lincoln had vigorously participated in every presidential canvass, and his campaign speeches show that he had developed very definite ideas about the proper role of the Chief Executive. During most of this time he was a Whig, and he always remained proud of his Whig record. During the Lincoln-Douglas debates he reminded his hearers of his Whig past: "In '32, I voted for Henry Clay, in '36 for the Hugh L. White ticket, in '40 for 'Tip and Tyler.' In '44 I made the last great effort for 'Old Harry of the West.' . . . Taylor was elected in '48, and we fought nobly for Scott in '52." The leaders of the Whig party were his heroes; Henry Clay, in particular, he "loved and revered as a teacher and leader." Proud of his Whig principles, Lincoln boasted that he "had stood by the party as long as it had a being." He did not like the idea of being "un-whigged," and only after the death of his old party did he, rather reluctantly, join the Republicans.

The party to which Lincoln belonged for most of his life originated in objections to the "executive usurpation" of Andrew Jackson. Whig leaders concealed their economic motives and personal aspirations under denunciation of Jackson as "a detestable, ignorant, reckless, vain and malignant tyrant." Just as their ancestors of 1776 had stood against another executive usurper, so the Whigs of the 1830's fought against the "dictator" in the White House. Henry Clay and Daniel Webster bewailed the policy of the Democrats, which was tending rapidly toward "a total change of the pure republican character of our government, and to the concentration of all power in the hands of one man." William Henry Harrison, the first Whig President, made his inaugural address a classic exposition of his party's creed: ". . . it is preposterous to suppose that . . . the President, placed at the capital, in the center of the country could better understand the wants and wishes of the people than their own immediate representatives who spend a part of every year among them . . . and [are] bound to them by the triple tie of interest, duty, and affection." Zachary Taylor, the only other President elected by the Whig party, held the same views: "The Executive . . .

has authority to recommend (not to dictate) measures to Congress. Having performed that duty, the Executive department of the Government cannot rightfully control the decision of Congress on any subject of legislation . . . the . . . veto will never be exercised by me except . . . as an extreme measure, to be resorted to only in extraordinary cases . . ."

Abraham Lincoln, a young Whig campaigner who regularly supported his party's ticket and platform, shared these fears of a strong executive. In 1838, in one of his earliest public lectures, he expressed concern lest "some man possessed of the loftiest genius, coupled with ambition sufficient to push it to its utmost stretch," some man belonging *"to the family of the lion, or the tribe of the eagle,"* seize executive leadership and "set boldly to the task of pulling down" the institutions of the free republic. Consequently he opposed all aggrandizement of the President's powers. The Democratic tendency to allow the President "to take the whole of legislation into his own hands" he branded "a most pernicious deception." He argued against President James K. Polk's "high-handed and despotic exercise of the veto power, and . . . utter disregard of the will of the people, in refusing to give assent to measures which their representatives passed for the good and prosperity of the country." Congress should make policy and the President should execute it. That was "the best sort of principle"; that was the basic democratic "principle of allowing the people to do as they please with their own business."

These arguments were not just campaign oratory, for Lincoln clung to them throughout his life. In 1861 on his way to Washington as President Elect, he announced that he did not believe the Chief Executive should recommend legislation to Congress, veto bills already passed, or exert "indirect influence to affect the action of congress." "My political education," he declared, "strongly inclines me against a very free use of any of these means, by the Executive, to control the legislation of the country. As a rule, I think it better that congress should originate, as well as perfect its measures, without external bias." On the controversial tariff issue, for instance, he thought the President should "neither seek to force a tariff-law by

Executive influence; nor yet to arrest a reasonable one, by a veto, or otherwise." Throughout the war he kept reminding his subordinates that the executive branch must not "expressly or impliedly seize and exercise the permanent legislative functions of the government."

Lincoln's curious failure to assert his control over his Cabinet also derived from his basic Whig view of the presidency. The Whig party was originally founded not only to oppose executive pressures upon the Congress but to combat the President's complete domination of the administrative offices. When President Jackson abruptly ousted two successive Secretaries of the Treasury in order to install a malleable third secretary who followed the President's will and removed Federal deposits from the Bank of the United States, the Whigs howled that he was subjecting the entire government to "*one responsibility, one discretion, one will.*" Whig President Harrison declared that the Founding Fathers should have made the head of the Treasury Department "entirely independent of the Executive," since the President should "never be looked to for schemes of finance." Other Whigs extended this reasoning to cover the rest of the Cabinet. Webster was only carrying Whig principles to their logical conclusion when he asserted that all measures of an administration should be brought before the Cabinet, where "their settlement was to be decided by the majority of votes, each member of the Cabinet and the President having but one vote."

Lincoln was, of course, too strong a personality to submit to such dictation. Indeed, even during the Taylor administration he had realized that the Whig theory of Cabinet responsibility gave "The President the . . . ruinous character of being a mere man of straw." Consequently, when Seward in April 1861 proposed to become virtual premier of the new administration in order to lead it on a daring new policy of foreign embroilments, Lincoln quietly squelched him, declaring: ". . . if this must be done, *I* must do it." Similarly, when preparing to issue the Emancipation Proclamation, Lincoln told his Cabinet advisers: "I have got you together to hear what I have written down. I do not wish your advice about the main matter—for that I have determined for myself . . . If there is anything in the expressions I use, or in any other minor matter, which anyone of you thinks had best be changed, I shall be glad to receive the suggestions."

On key policies, therefore, especially those involving the use of the war power, Lincoln, like Harrison and Taylor before him, departed from the Whig theory of Cabinet responsibility, but he could not rid himself of the political ideas with which he had been raised. Given the alternatives of imposing his own will upon his Cabinet or of submitting to their majority opinion, Lincoln evaded the decision by treating the Cabinet as a necessary nuisance, allowing it to consider only insignificant matters. Since there was no real consultation to formulate common policy and since the President could not personally oversee the details of everyday administration, each secretary, however disagreeable, self-promoting, or even conspiratorial, had a free hand in conducting his own department's affairs.

IV

THESE WEAKNESSES of Lincoln's administration seem to stand in sharp contrast with the President's energetic assertion of his powers over civil liberties, over the military forces, and over the rebellious South, but there is no evidence that Lincoln himself was troubled by any inconsistency in his roles. Necessity, not political theory, caused him to make his first sweeping assertions of executive authority during the secession crisis. The onset of civil war posed the immediate, practical dilemma, he declared later, "whether, using only the existing means, agencies, and processes which Congress had provided, I should let the government fall at once into ruin, or whether, availing myself of the broader powers conferred by the Constitution in cases of insurrection, I would make an effort to save it with all its blessings for the present age and for posterity." When the question was so posed, the answer became simple. "Necessity knows no law," he thought; consequently it was obligatory for him in this crisis to take strong measures, "some of which," he admitted, "were without any authority of law," in order to save the government.

When it did become necessary for Lincoln to justify his actions, he found his defense in the war powers granted him under the Constitution. ". . . as Commander in Chief of the Army and Navy, in time of war," he asserted, "I suppose I have a right to take any measure which may best subdue the enemy." Though critics claimed that the President was asserting dictatorial authority, it is clear that Lincoln himself took a narrower view of his powers. For example, he rejected the application of a general to construct a railroad in Missouri, which, it was claimed, would have some military utility. Since real military necessity was not shown, Lincoln felt this was an unwarranted extension of executive power. ". . . I have been," he assured Congress, "unwilling to go beyond the pressure of necessity in the unusual exercise of power."

The complex problem of emancipation shows the degree to which Lincoln's conception of his war powers served both as a source for executive action and as a restriction upon such action. His personal preferences, the expediencies of politics, the thundering pressure from Northern governors, and the growing sentiment that emancipation would aid the Union cause abroad all urged him during 1861 and 1862 to move against slavery. He delayed, not because he doubted his constitutional power, but because he questioned the necessity. "The truth is," he told a Louisiana loyalist, "that what is done, and omitted, about slaves, is done and omitted on the same military necessity." By late 1862 when necessity clearly demanded the abolition of slavery, Lincoln issued his proclamation of freedom, "as Commander in Chief, of the Army and Navy of the United States in time of actual armed rebellion against authority and government of the United States, and as a fit and necessary war measure for suppressing said rebellion." The Emancipation Proclamation, he declared later, had "no constitutional or legal justification, except as a military measure."

This view that the Chief Executive possesses vast war powers is not necessarily in conflict with the Whig view of the presidency. To be sure, the Whiggish origins of Lincoln's thought on this problem are not so clearly demonstrable. The Whig party had originated in opposition to a strong President. Only two Presidents were ever elected by the Whig party, and neither of them was in the White House during time of war. Consequently, men like Webster and Clay spoke more of the limitation of presidential power in peacetime than they did of its possible wartime expansion. Lincoln himself had shared these preoccupations of his party leaders. Vigorously he denounced Democratic President Polk, who, he believed, had unjustly and unconstitutionally started the Mexican War by invading foreign territory. The argument "that if it shall become *necessary, to repel invasion*, the President, may without violation of the Constitution . . . *invade* the territory of another country" Lincoln rejected as permitting the Chief Executive "to make war at pleasure" and as subjecting the American people to "the most oppressive of all Kingly oppressions." But though he opposed the Mexican War, neither Lincoln nor his party leaders made serious objections to President Polk's vigorous assertion of his war powers once the conflict had begun.

Whigs were inhibited from making such an objection. Heirs of the Federalists, they were at heart strong nationalists. One important current of Whig thought in fact justified the broadest assertion of presidential powers in wartime. Its most articulate exponent was John Quincy Adams, who, though far too independent and cantankerous to give his undivided allegiance to any party, acted generally with the Whigs in his distinguished postpresidential career in the House of Representatives. In congressional debates in 1836, 1841, and 1842, Adams, as he proudly recorded in his diary, "stung the slavocracy to madness" by sketching in sweeping terms the power of the President as commander in chief. "[B]y the laws of war," he reminded his listeners, "an invaded country has all its laws and municipal institutions swept by the board, and martial law takes the place of them." In case of "actual war, whether servile, civil, or foreign," he grimly told Congress, the South's "municipal institutions" would be entirely subject to these laws of war, which permitted the confiscation of enemy property, including slaves. Consequently, in such an event, "not only the President of the United States but the commander of the army has the power to order the universal emancipation of the slaves."

Though John Quincy Adams could never have been considered the spokesman for any party, a respectable body of Whig thinkers endorsed these views. It is significant that the strongest defender of Lincoln's power to suspend the writ of habeas corpus was the venerable Whig lawyer Horace Binney, of Philadelphia, who saw no inconsistency between this position and his condemnation of Jackson's "tyranny" during the 1830's. Another former Whig, William Whiting of Massachusetts, provided in 1862 an even broader defense of the President's powers as commander in chief. His booklet on *The War Powers of the President*, which went through forty-three editions during the decade after its publication, leaned heavily upon Adams's argument, which he claimed proved "in the amplest terms the powers of Congress, and the authority of the President, to free enemy's slaves, as a legitimate act of war." An old Democrat like Gideon Welles distrusted Whiting's ideas and sneered at him as "self-sufficient but superficial, with many words, some reading, but no very sound or well-founded political views," but Lincoln, who shared the lawyer's Whig background, said flatly: "I like Mr. Whiting very much . . . ," and made him Solicitor of the War Department.

Since the Whigs were generally out of office and always on the defensive, John Quincy Adams's doctrine of presidential war powers never became an official part of the party's creed, but it was not forgotten. When the Civil War came, it was the ex-Whig Horace Greeley who revived Adams's speech on the presidential power of emancipation and gave it generous space in his New York *Tribune*. Another former Whig, Senator Charles Sumner of Massachusetts, who regarded Adams's argument "as a towering landmark and beacon," welcomed the firing on Fort Sumter because it introduced just the contingency the ex-President had forecast. As soon as he heard the news, Sumner said: "I went at once to Mr. Lincoln . . . and told him I was with him now heart and soul; that under the war power the right had come to him to emancipate the slaves."

V

THUS what Lincoln called his "political education" helps explain the puzzling ambiguity of his presidency. Both in strongly asserting his war powers and in weakly deferring to Congress, he was following the Whig creed in which he was raised.

So to interpret Lincoln's course is to give more significance to the Whig party and its ideology than is fashionable among historians today. Concerned with showing that our major political parties have generally shared most of their basic ideas, recent scholars have belittled the political rivalries of the 1830's and 1840's as inconsequential struggles between conflicting economic interest groups or contests between ambitious politicians. Doubtless, in the backward glance of history, there is much justification for such an interpretation. But it must be remembered that what men think to be true often has more influence upon the course of history than actuality itself.

To the generation of American politicians who reached maturity about 1840 the difference between the Whig party and the Democratic party was a real and vital thing. Young and aspiring leaders like Abraham Lincoln who shouted themselves hoarse for rival party candidates convinced themselves, even if they convinced nobody else, that the principles which they advocated were both true and important. Rhetoric has a way of imprisoning those who use it, and the politicians of the Civil War era were never quite able to discard the party creeds of their youth. Lincoln, in other connections, recognized the danger of letting past experience dictate present action. "As our case is new," he argued, "so we must think anew, and act anew." But the President was never able to disenthrall himself from his own political education. It is ironical that the Whig party, which had a sorry record of failure during its lifetime, should have achieved its greatest success, years after its official demise, in the presidency of Abraham Lincoln.

ELEVEN

Reverence for the Laws: Abraham Lincoln and the Founding Fathers

OF THE MANY ESSAYS BY the late J. G. Randall, long the dean of Lincoln scholars, one of the most interesting is "The Rule of Law Under Lincoln." A great admirer of Abraham Lincoln, Professor Randall was also a profound student of constitutional and legal history, and this brief essay shows that he was torn between his respect for the historical discipline in which he had been trained and his affection for the great Civil War President. In this essay the tension was not resolved, and his discussion of the rule of law under Lincoln became, despite Randall's intentions, a catalogue of the numerous ways in which law did *not* rule during the Civil War years.

I

JUDGING FROM LINCOLN'S PRE–CIVIL WAR RECORD, one would have expected him to be a President who meticulously observed the law and followed the Constitution. After all, he was himself a lawyer, one of great experience and considerable distinction. The popular image of Abraham Lincoln as an untutored country lawyer, who relied more on his native wit and common sense than on legal learning, is a myth. He was, instead, an incredibly hardworking lawyer. The Lincoln Legal Papers in Springfield has recently collected a vast array of documents covering the thousands of cases in which he participated. In nearly all of these he wrote out all the papers in his own hand, and sometimes this involved enormous labor. In the 1855 Macoupin County case of *Clark & Morrison* v. *Page & Bacon,* which involved the claims of some St. Louis bankers and financiers, Lincoln for the defendants drafted a forty-three-page answer to the plaintiff's bill of complaints; this was a task that required immense concentration, and Lincoln's handwriting suggests that he wrote the entire document at one sitting. Of course few cases required so much labor, but Lincoln's clients rarely lost a suit because of carelessness or inattention on the part of their attorney. His cases before the Illinois Supreme Court and the federal district courts involved considerable research in the well-stocked State Library and the Supreme Court Library, which had the reports of all the state supreme courts and the federal courts, as well as the usual legal reference works and dictionaries. Even in highly technical cases involving patents and railroad rights Lincoln looked up the authorities and cited them in the elaborate briefs he wrote out by hand, outlining the principal issues before the court.

Lincoln was proud of his profession. Of course he took pleasure from time to time in making fun of lawyers and of telling some of his celebrated "leetle stories" about them. One of his favorites was of the young attorney in Sangamon County who hung out his shingle for a long time without having a client. When finally one came, he was very anxious not to lose his first case, so he went informally to the justice of the peace to learn how he would probably decide it. After hearing the argument the young man intended to present in court the next day, the justice of the peace told him: "As you state the case, I should be obliged to decide against you. But you had better bring the case. Probably the other side will make so much worse a showing that I shall have to decide the case in your favor." But mostly Lincoln took the law, and lawyers, very seriously. A lecture he prepared for young Springfield attorneys was notable not just because it urged diligence, careful preparation, and clear public speaking but because it enjoined his listeners to avoid even the appearance of dishonesty: "Resolve to be honest at all events; and if, in your own judgment, you can not be an honest lawyer, resolve to be honest without being a lawyer."

Along with pride in his profession went respect for the government under which the legal system operated. Lincoln revered the Declaration of Independence and the Constitution as the basic documents upon which American democracy rested. For the framers of these documents, whom he called "iron men," he expressed veneration approaching awe. George Washington, that "mightiest name of earth," was such a majestic figure that Lincoln resorted to uncharacteristic rhetorical excess in characterizing him: "To add brightness to the sun or glory to the name of Washington is alike impossible." He paid tribute to John Adams, Benjamin Franklin, Alexander Hamilton, and others of the revolutionary generation, but for none was his admiration so great as Thomas Jefferson, whom he called "the most distinguished politician of our history," whose principles were "the definitions and axioms of free society."

"I have never had a feeling politically that did not spring from the sentiments embodied in the Declaration of Independence," Lincoln declared. Jefferson's proclamation that all men are created equal—and sometimes Lincoln misquoted and said the Declaration proclaimed all men free and equal—was the basis for American society. But it was even more. The Declaration of Independence, that *"immortal emblem of Humanity,"* was "the electric cord . . . that links the hearts of patriotic and liberty-loving men together . . . as long as the love of freedom exists in the minds of men throughout the world." It reached out to people of all races and nationalities and "erected a beacon to guide their children and their children's children, and the countless myriads who should inhabit the earth in other ages."

This reverence for the founders of the American government caused Lincoln as a young man to deplore proposals to amend the Constitution. "As a general rule, I think, we would [do] much better [to] let it alone. No slight occasion should tempt us to touch it."

He made it his rule that "if we would supplant the opinions and policy of our fathers in any case, we should do so upon evidence so conclusive, and argument so clear, that even their great authority, fairly considered and weighed, cannot stand." He accorded the same respect to decisions of the courts and to laws enacted under the Constitution. Of course, he said, "bad laws, if they exist, should be repealed as soon as possible, still while they continue in force, for the sake of example, they should be religiously observed."

A natural conservative, Lincoln was disturbed by the evidence of social disintegration that he saw in American society, as mob rule and vigilantism indicated "the growing disposition to substitute the wild and furious passions, in lieu of the sober judgement of Courts." In an early lecture he asked how the country could be protected. His answer was simple: "Let every American, every lover of liberty, every well wisher to his posterity, swear by the blood of the Revolution, never to violate in the least particular, the laws of the country; and never to tolerate their violation by others." "Let reverence for the laws, be breathed by every American mother, to the lisping babe, that prattles on her lap," he urged, "let it be taught in schools, in seminaries, and in colleges. . . . And, in short, let it become the *political religion* of the nation."

II

THE RECORD OF LINCOLN'S PRESIDENTIAL YEARS seems in sharp contrast to Lincoln's earlier undeviating insistence on reverence for the Constitution and obedience to the laws. Immediately after his inauguration, Lincoln confronted the crisis over Fort Sumter. Once the Confederates opened fire, he responded quickly and, invoking "the power in me vested by the Constitution, and the laws," called up 75,000 members of the state militias to put down an armed insurrection "too powerful to be suppressed by the ordinary course of judicial proceedings." To supplement this action, which was undoubtedly within his prerogative as President, he ordered the expansion of the regular United States army by ten additional regiments and the enlistment of 18,000 men in the navy. To protect ships from California bearing gold so necessary for Union finances, he dispatched an armed revenue cutter, and he ordered the commandants at the navy yards at Boston, New York, and Philadelphia each to purchase and arm five steamships in order to preserve water communication with Washington. In case that communication was temporarily cut off by the Confederates, he authorized Governor E. D. Morgan of New York and an associate to act for the United States government in forwarding troops and supplies. He also directed the Treasury Department to advance, without requiring security, $2,000,000 to a New York committee headed by John A. Dix to pay "such requisitions as should be directly consequent upon the military and naval measures necessary for the defence and support of the government." For none of these measures did he have congressional authorization. "Whether strictly legal or not," he said later, they "were ventured upon, under what appeared to be a popular demand and a public necessity; trusting . . . that Congress would readily ratify them."

At the same time Lincoln curbed civil liberties. As secessionist mobs went on the rampage in Baltimore and blocked the passage of federal troops to Washington, the President suspended the privilege of the writ of habeas corpus along the route through Maryland. That action meant that Federal commanders in the region could arrest and imprison without charges persons whom they suspected of disloyalty. Persons thus imprisoned had no recourse. Under ordinary procedures they, or their attorneys, would secure a writ of habeas corpus from the appropriate federal court, and the arresting official would have to produce their prisoners and bring specific charges against them. But now, with the suspension of the great writ, army officers were commanded to ignore all such judicial proceedings. The Chief Justice of the United States, Roger Brooke Taney, protested that the suspension of the writ of habeas corpus meant "the people of the United States are no longer living under a government of laws; but every citizen holds life, liberty and property at the will and pleasure of the army officer in whose military district he may happen to be found," and he reminded the President of his oath to "take care that the laws be faithfully executed." But Lincoln had little respect for the Supreme Court after the Dred Scott decision, and he no longer believed that even bad laws should be obeyed. He simply ignored Taney's protest and presently extended the suspension of the writ. By the fall of 1862 the suspension covered the entire North. The number of individuals who suffered from such arbitrary arrests throughout the war remains unknown; after years of the most laborious research, Mark E. Neely, in his Pulitzer Prize–winning study *The Fate of Liberty*, places it as well in excess of 16,000.

Over other basic civil liberties the Lincoln administration exercised looser control. There was no concerted attempt to control freedom of speech among civilians, but public expressions of hostility to the war, especially when they were designed to discourage recruitment of Union troops or to foster desertion, met swift punishment. There was no general censorship of the press, though from time to time individual newspapers were suppressed—usually only for short periods of time—when they carried forbidden military news or actively promoted disloyalty. Thus the Chicago *Times* was briefly suspended because of "disloyal and incendiary sentiments." When the New York *World* and the *Journal of Commerce*, in an attempt to rig the stock market, published a bogus proclamation by the President calling for 400,000 additional troops and appointing a national day of public humiliation and prayer, these papers were also punished by brief suspensions.

President Lincoln's far-ranging activities extended to the very structure of government. Gone now was his earlier reluctance to tamper with the text of the Constitution; he enthusiastically promoted the adoption of the Thirteenth Amendment ending slavery. As Union armies advanced, he took control of state governments in the South. The President appointed "provisional governors"—an office unknown to the Constitution and unauthorized by the Congress—to supervise the reconstruction of these former Confederate states. To the officials entrusted with the reorganization of conquered Louisiana, Lincoln gave blunt advice: "Follow forms of law as far as convenient. . . ."

So sweeping was Lincoln's exercise of power in ways never before used by an American President and not authorized by the Congress that his opponents called him a dictator. Even Professor Randall was obliged to admit that "No President has carried the power of presidential edict and executive order (independently of Congress) so far as he did."

III

THE PICTURE OF ABRAHAM LINCOLN in the prewar years as an unqualified supporter of "reverence for the laws" and that of President Lincoln who told his subordinates to follow the "forms of law as far as convenient" seem entirely inconsistent, and historians have struggled to find ways to reconcile the two images.

One approach, which has considerable merit, is to adopt Lincoln's own explanation that his extralegal and perhaps unconstitutional actions were responses to dire necessity. Claiming to be "thoroughly imbued with a reverence for the guaranteed rights of individuals," the President said that he abridged these rights only when it became "indispensable to the public safety." Facing "a clear, flagrant, and gigantic case of rebellion," he had no choice but to take "measures, otherwise unconstitutional," which he believed "might become lawful, by becoming indispensable to the preservation of the constitution, through the preservation of the nation." He had no fear, he said, that he was setting a bad precedent. To argue "that the American people will, by means of military arrests during the Rebellion, lose the right of Public Discussion, the Liberty of Speech and the Press, the Law of Evidence, Trial by Jury, and Habeas Corpus, through the indefinite peaceful future" was like claiming "that a man could contract so strong an appetite for emetics during temporary illness as to persist in feeding upon them during the remainder of his healthful life."

This argument has plausibility. At the outbreak of the Civil War the Union government was left so defenseless that some emergency actions had to be taken. If increasing the size of the regular army or entrusting federal funds to loyal agents in New York were irregular procedures, these were realistic responses to genuine dangers. Admitting that he took such measures, "whether strictly legal or not," in response to "a popular demand and a public necessity," Lincoln defended them, saying that he had done "nothing... beyond the constitutional competency of Congress," and he correctly anticipated that the legislative body when it assembled would ratify what he had done.

But other infringements of civil liberties under the Lincoln administration are more difficult to justify on the grounds of necessity. It is not clear an emergency warranted the suspension of the writ of habeas corpus throughout the Northern states. Allegedly Lincoln acted to crush disloyalty and to put down incipient rebellion, especially in the Ohio Valley region, but the nature and extent of Northern disaffection toward the Union cause are subjects on which historians disagree. For many years the standard account was Wood Gray's *The Hidden Civil War*, which gave full credit to talk of Copperhead conspiracies throughout the North and to threats of revolt in the Middle West and thus justified arbitrary action to crush incipient Northern rebellion. But more recently Frank Klement and Kenneth M. Stampp have more closely re-examined the so-called Copperhead movement and have found it essentially an arm of the Democratic party, which was certainly antiadministration but generally strongly pro-Union. The often hysterical reports of the Northern Republican war Governors were political pronouncements designed to keep their party in office.

Certainly their reports deeply troubled Lincoln, who was normally unflappable. By 1863 he told Massachusetts Senator Charles Sumner that he now feared "'the fire in the rear'—meaning the Democracy especially at the North West—more than our military chances," and his administration intervened to crush the Copperhead movement. Newspapers that attacked the government or seemed to discourage enlistments were suppressed. Provost marshals in the West made sweeps of the disaffected, jailing many and invoking Lincoln's suspension of the writ of habeas corpus to deny them trial. The most notorious case occurred in May 1863, when former Ohio Congressman Clement L. Vallandigham was arrested for declaring that the Lincoln administration had needlessly prolonged the war in order to liberate the blacks and enslave the whites in America. Convicted by a military tribunal, Vallandigham was sentenced to spend the rest of the war in a military prison.

If such actions were in response to a largely imaginary danger, it is hard to defend the claim that necessity compelled President Lincoln to suspend the rule of law.

IV

ANOTHER WAY to reconcile the conflicting images of Lincoln the upholder of law with Lincoln the lawbreaker is to minimize the importance and frequency of the extralegal transgressions during his presidential years, and this also is a reasonable argument. It is easy to point out the numerous actions that Lincoln did *not* take to infringe the political and civil liberties of citizens. For instance, the President made no attempt to interfere with, or postpone, state and local elections, even when it was clear that they would go against him and his party. A true dictator would never have permitted the midterm congressional elections of 1862, right after the Emancipation Proclamation, when public opinion was running strongly in favor of the Democrats. Certainly Lincoln was very anxious over the outcome of these elections. A Chicago woman who visited him at this time remarked that he seemed "literally bending under the weight of his burdens," and said that "his introverted look and his half-staggering gait were like those of a man walking in sleep," while his face "revealed the ravages which care, anxiety, and overwork had wrought." The huge gains made by the Democrats in congressional and gubernatorial elections in New York, Pennsylvania, New Jersey, Ohio, Indiana, and Illinois, led the New York *Times* to observe that the election had been a "vote of want of confidence" in the Lincoln administration. But the President made no move to overrule the results.

Similarly in 1864, when Lincoln's own re-election was at stake, he never considered postponing or canceling the presidential election. Even if that had been constitutionally possible, he said, "the election was a necessity." "We can not have free government without elections," he explained; "and if the rebellion could force us to forego, or postpone a national election, it might fairly claim to have already conquered and ruined us." The Democratic nomination of General George B. McClellan posed a formidable threat, not just to Lincoln's own prospects but to the success of the Union cause, and as late as August Lincoln concluded that "it seems exceedingly probable that the Administration will not be re-elected." But the President did nothing to change the rules to prevent that likely outcome. He did not, for example, attempt to rush through Congress a bill admitting the new states of Colorado and Nebraska, both of which would have voted for his re-election, nor did he try to force the readmission of Louisiana, Tennessee, and other Southern states, partially reconstructed but still under military control, which would surely have added to his electoral strength.

In addition, it has to be stressed that, though there were occasional infringements of freedom of the press, Lincoln never called for, or instituted, any nationwide censorship. There was no attempt to suppress scurrilous Democratic pamphlets like *The Lincoln Catechism*, which called the President "Abraham Africanus the First" and said Lincoln's own Ten Commandments began: "Thou shall have no other God but the negro."

Even in the matter of arbitrary arrests recent scholarship shows that the transgressions of the Lincoln administration may have been exaggerated. Mark E. Neely, Jr., have proved that most persons thus arrested were citizens of the Confederacy or pro-Confederate citizens of the border states. Of the rest, a majority consisted of blockade runners, draft evaders, smugglers, spies for the Confederacy, swindlers of recruits, and other common criminals. In most of these cases the suspension of the writ of habeas corpus was required to enforce the laws against common criminals in a time of great social unrest.

But after such allowances have been made, the fact remains that civil liberties were abridged under the Lincoln administration. About one thousand Northerners were held as prisoners of state during the Civil War—a number large enough to exercise a chilling influence on dissent and on freedom of expression in the entire population.

V

A THIRD WAY to reconcile Lincoln's reverence for the laws and his apparent disregard for those laws is to put the blame for infringements of civil liberties on the President's lieutenants rather than on Lincoln himself. Once again there is something to be said for this point of view. Lincoln's subordinates were more willing than the President to curb civil liberties, and some of them were less than discreet in describing their activities. Secretary of State William H. Seward, who supervised all political prisoners during the early months of the war, appeared to rejoice in his unrestrained power. Allegedly he told Lord Lyons, the British minister in Washington, that he could arrest a citizen anywhere in the United States merely by ringing a little bell on his desk. Could even the Queen of England do that? he asked. Later, when Secretary of War Edwin M. Stanton was put in charge, he seemed actually to enjoy showing a tough-minded indifference to personal liberties, and some military commanders callously disregarded the rights of civilians.

But before absolving the President from responsibility it would be well to take a closer look at the Vallandigham case, the most notorious political arrest during the Civil War. The ex-Congressman was arrested at the order of General Ambrose P. Burnside. Fresh from his defeat at Fredericksburg, Burnside, now commander of the Department of the Ohio, was determined that no carelessness on his part should lead to further disaster, and he was resolved to crush out what he called "treason, expressed or implied," in his department. He issued an order threatening to arrest anyone who was in "the habit of declaring sympathies for the enemy." When Vallandigham denounced the order, Burnside had him seized, imprisoned, and tried before a military tribunal.

Before putting all the blame on Burnside, it is well to remember that, as Lincoln freely admitted, the President was ultimately responsible for his subordinate's actions. After all, Lincoln had appointed this incompetent and politically insensitive general to his command. Further, Burnside did not act entirely on his own initiative. He issued his order after studying Lincoln's proclamation of September 24, 1862, which suspended the writ of habeas corpus throughout the North, and he sent his edict to Washington, where neither Lincoln nor the war department disapproved of it. When Burnside went on to arrest Vallandigham, he promptly notified the White House, and Lincoln, though he had little information about the case and no time to judge its political impact, telegraphed the general his "kind assurance of support."

To be sure, after the President learned more about the case, he had second thoughts. "It gave me pain when I learned that Mr. Vallandigham had been arrested," he said a few months later, and he declared frankly that, acting "in my own discretion, I do not know whether I would have ordered the arrest." He tried to mitigate the stiff sentence of imprisonment in a military jail by commuting it to exile behind the Confederate lines; and when Vallandigham promptly left the Confederacy for Canada and, in a Falstaffian disguise, crossed back into Ohio in order to run as Democratic candidate for governor of that state, Lincoln quietly ignored these open violations of his sentence. But such leniency stemmed from political expediency, not from an instinctive outrage at the violation of the civil rights of an American citizen.

In all such cases Lincoln acted from his fixed conviction that the Union must be preserved whatever the immediate costs to individuals or to traditional liberties. This was evident from the earliest days of the war. In April 1861, right after the firing on Fort Sumter, he feared that the Maryland legislature might assemble and try to take that state out of the Union, and he authorized General Winfield Scott to prevent it from meeting. Though the danger, as it proved, was imaginary, Lincoln told the general to take any steps required, including the suspension of the writ of habeas corpus and, "if necessary, . . . the bombardment of their cities."

That grim determination persisted throughout the war. For example, in the fall of 1863, when Lincoln learned that Emerson Etheridge, the clerk of the House of Representatives, planned to take advantage of a technicality and throw the organization of the House into the hands of the Democratic minority, Lincoln not merely monitored the situation closely and urged all Republican members to be present on the day the House first met. He went further to pledge that if Etheridge persisted in his scheme he would "be carried out on a chip," and he promised to have a troop of soldiers ready to assist.

Of course Lincoln was a kindly man, genuinely opposed to oppressive measures, and he did not enjoy causing hardship. From time to time he welcomed occasions to intervene on the side of generosity and civil rights—especially in widely publicized cases where his intervention would cause favorable comment and reinforce his image as Father Abraham, the genial, if sometimes necessarily stern, father of his country. But such interventions were exceptional. In general, the record shows that the preservation of civil liberties was never the primary concern of the Lincoln administration.

VI

BEFORE DISCARDING LINCOLN'S PRAISE for the rule of law as rhetoric that was discarded once he came to power, it would be well to consider Lincoln's wartime actions as the application of his political philosophy, which derived from his view of the Constitution and the men who framed it.

Lincoln had very carefully studied the speeches and writings of the founding fathers. Nowhere is this more evident than in his Cooper Union Address of 1860, written at a time when he was much occupied with legal cases and was preparing to run for the presidential nomination. Closely, and quite accurately, he analyzed the public and private expressions of the thirty-nine men who signed the Constitution, with a view of determining their position on congressional control over slavery in the territories. As a piece of historical research it remains highly creditable, and it demonstrates how thoroughly immersed Lincoln was in the political ideas of the Revolutionary generation.

Unlike many constitutional experts of his time, Lincoln did not make a distinction between the framers of the Constitution and the signers of the Declaration of Independence. He did not see the two documents as being in conflict, nor did he think the Constitution was in any sense a conservative reaction to the radicalism of the Declaration. The two great American charters, he declared, were "the work of the same generation of men . . . who declared independence—who fought the war of the revolution—who afterwards made the constitution under which we still live." In his mind the Constitution fulfilled the promises of the Declaration, the basic document on which his political philosophy rested.

In making this linkage Lincoln was dissenting from the constitutional theory that had dominated American jurisprudence since the Jacksonian era. Jurists of this persuasion tended to dismiss the Declaration of Independence as essentially a rhetorical exercise, and they adopted a narrow, technical interpretation of the Constitution that stressed the limitations on the powers of the Federal government. This was the constitutional view that enabled South Carolina's John C. Calhoun to construct his schemes of checks and balances to curb what he feared would be the tyranny of the majority; it was the set of ideas behind Chief Justice Taney's opinion in the Dred Scott case, denying Congress any power over slavery in the national territories; and it was the body of doctrine that caused President James Buchanan, even while he lamented the secession of the Deep South, to declare that the national government could do nothing to prevent it.

But this was not, and never had been, the only way of looking at the basic charter on which the American government was founded. The Federalists saw the Constitution as a potent engine for social and economic change, and their spokesman, Chief Justice John Marshall, daringly asserted powers for the national government even at a time when the Jacksonian Democracy sought to devolve them on the states. Justice Joseph Story, whose influential commentaries on the Constitution helped shape the ideas of generations of Northern lawyers, continued this nationalist tradition, as did Daniel Webster and other leading Whigs. They insisted that the Constitution was never meant to be an iron hoop girdling the trunk of the tree of nationalism. Instead, as one Whig theorist put it, it should be viewed as "the tree itself, — native to the soil that bore it, — waxing strong in sunshine and in storm, putting forth branches, leaves, and roots, according to the laws of its own growth, and flourishing with eternal verdure."

Lincoln's political thought was less figurative, but, as a dedicated Whig, he was thoroughly familiar with this body of legal doctrine that favored the use of government as an instrument of social policy. When the war came he drew on it, and, reinforced by the opinions of his attorney-general, Edward Bates, and his solicitor general, William Whiting, he used it as the basis for his conduct of the presidency. His expansive view of the war powers of the President was neither idiosyncratic nor unsupported. To forceful and learned commentators like Whiting, James Russell Lowell, Horace Binney, and Theophilus Parsons the President's actions seemed exactly what was required by the Constitutional provision that the national government must provide for the general welfare. Many of these publicists argued, as did Lincoln, that the President's expansive view of his war powers over internal subversion and over the reorganization of the Southern states was authorized by the constitutional provision requiring the national government to guarantee to every state a republican form of government. And most of them, like Lincoln, looked to the Declaration of Independence to reinforce these constitutional provisions. These jurists argued that constitutions and bills of rights should no longer be viewed as limitations on public authority but as sources of power and of liberty.

Denounced during the war by strict-constructionist commentators, usually from the Democratic party, and largely ignored in the postwar laissez-faire era, this expansive interpretation of the Constitution was long neglected by historians until Harold M. Hyman, William M. Wiecek, and Phillip S. Paludan revived this strong and legitimate nationalist interpretation. Today, these scholars observe, this view would be called "instrumentalism," but in the Civil War years it was more frequently labeled an "adequacy-of-the-Constitution" interpretation.

This was the legal theory on which Lincoln freely drew. He saw the emergency powers he assumed during the war years as a fulfillment, not an abandonment, of the rule of law. In his mind there was no contradiction between the actions he felt obliged to take in order to defend the Constitution and the spirit of that document, because his oath of office imposed on him "the duty of preserving, by every indispensable means, that government—that nation—of which that constitution was the organic law." Only by preserving the nation could he insure that the political religion of the United States should continue to be "reverence for the laws."

TWELVE

A. Lincoln, Politician

I

THE STATESMANSHIP of Abraham Lincoln is so widely recognized as to require no defense. But it is not always realized that Lincoln's opportunities for statesmanship were made possible by his accomplishments as a politician. Perhaps it is too cynical to say that a statesman is a politician who succeeds in getting himself elected President. Still, but for his election in 1860, Lincoln's name would appear in our history books as that of a minor Illinois politician who unsuccessfully debated with Stephen A. Douglas. And had the President been defeated in 1864, he would be written off as one of the great failures of the American political system—the man who let his country drift into civil war, presided aimlessly over a graft-ridden administration, conducted an incompetent and ineffectual attempt to subjugate the Southern states, and after four years was returned by the people to the obscurity that he so richly deserved.

Lincoln's fame, then, was made possible by his success as a politician, yet in many of the techniques used by present-day political leaders he was singularly ineffectual. He never succeeded in selling himself—to the press, to the politicians, or to the people. To a public-relations expert, the Lincoln story would seem a gift from heaven. Like a skillful organist playing upon the keyboard of popular emotion, he could pull out the sentimental tremolo for Lincoln's humble origins, for his hardscrabble Kentucky and Indiana childhood, for his Illinois rise from rags to respectability. A good publicity man would emphasize Lincoln's sense of humor (but, as a recent campaign has demonstrated, he should not overemphasize it), his down-to-earth folksiness, his sympathy for the oppressed. Appealing to the traditional American love of a fighter, especially an underdog, he could capitalize upon the virulent assaults of Lincoln's political enemies. The whole campaign, if managed by a Batten, Barton, Durstine & Osborn agent, should have been as appealing, as saccharine, as successful as Richard Nixon's famous 1952 television appearance.

In Lincoln's case, however, astonishingly little use was made of these sure-fire appeals—and when they were used, they backfired. The President said that he was a man of humble origins—and his opponents declared that, as Southern poor white trash, he was still cowed by the slaveholders and afraid of vigorously prosecuting the war. Lincoln stressed his sense of humor—and even his supporters protested: ". . . I do wish Abraham would tell fewer dirty stories." Mrs. Lincoln regularly visited the wounded in Washington's hospitals—and hostile newspapers hinted that she was really passing along military secrets to the Confederates.

Lincoln never succeeded in making his own case clear. He had no sounding-board. While Congressmen orated in the Capitol, the President sat gagged in the White House. In the 1860's, convention had it that a President must pretend not to be a politician. After wire-pulling for a lifetime to secure the nomination, the successful candidate must be surprised when a committee from his party officially notified him that he was the lucky man. In the campaign that followed, he was supposed to sit indifferently at home, pretending to be a Cincinnatus at the plow, while his fellow citizens, unsolicited, offered him the highest post in the land. And, once in the Executive Mansion, he was to be muffled and dumb.

Like most self-made men, Abraham Lincoln was very conventional, and he never challenged the rules of the political game. A strict view of the proprieties prevented President Lincoln from going directly to the people. Although he had made his fame as a public speaker, he never once addressed the Congress in person, but, following Jefferson's example, submitted written messages that dreary clerks droned out to apathetic legislators. Rarely after 1861 did Lincoln make any speeches or public pronouncements. "In my present position," he told a Maryland crowd in 1862, "it is hardly proper for me to make speeches." Later, as candidate for re-election, Lincoln still further limited his utterances. "I do not really think," he said in June 1864, "it is proper in my position for me to make a political speech. . . ." ". . . I believe it is not customary for one holding the office, and being a candidate for re-election, to do so. . . ." During the four years of civil war, the people could hear every strident and raucous voice in America, but not the voice of their President.

The President's negative attitude discouraged support from the press. Although he gave a number of informal interviews, Lincoln held no press conferences; reporters were still not considered quite respectable, certainly not worthy of private audience with the President. Newspapermen go where there is news. When a Washington correspondent found the White House well dry, he turned naturally to those running streams of gossip and complaint and criticism and intrigue, the Congressmen, whose anti-Lincoln pronouncements all too often agreed with the prejudices of his editor. Most of the leading American newspapers were anti-Lincoln in 1860, and they remained anti-Lincoln until April 15, 1865, when they suddenly discovered that the President had been the greatest man in the world. There were some notable exceptions, of course—the Springfield *Republican* and the New York *Times*, for example—but even these were handicapped by Lincoln's negative attitude toward the press. As one editor complained: ". . . it is our great desire to sustain the President, and we deplore the opportunity he has let go by, to sustain himself."

But most newspapers had no desire whatever to sustain the President, and they berated Lincoln with virulent obscenity. The sixteenth President was abused in the newspapers as "a slang-whanging stump speaker," a "half-witted usurper," a "mole-eyed" monster with "soul . . . of leather," "the present turtle at the head of the government," "the head ghoul at Washington."

President Lincoln was no more successful with the politicians than with the press. One of the saddest aspects of Civil War history is the sorry failure of Lincoln's appeals for bipartisan support. The Copperheads, outright antiwar Democrats, he could not hope to win, but the enormous mass of the Democratic party was as loyal to the Union as the President himself. On all crucial issues Lincoln was closer to George B. McClellan or Horatio Seymour than to many members of his own party. "In this time of national peril," Lincoln kept saying to such War Democrats, he hoped to meet them "upon a level one step higher than any party platform." He did not expect them to endorse every measure of a Republican regime, but he did wish that "'the Government' [might] be supported though the administration may not in every case wisely act." So earnestly did he desire the support of an energetic War Democrat like Governor Seymour of New York that in 1862 he sent him a message: if the Governor would help "wheel the Democratic party into line, put down rebellion, and preserve the government," Lincoln said, "I shall cheerfully make way for him as my successor."

Such hopes for bipartisan cooperation were blighted at birth. Governor Seymour regarded Lincoln's offer as a trap, and he spent most of his term in Albany denouncing the corruption and the arbitrary methods of the Lincoln administration. Far from cooperating, Democratic politicians took out time to compare Lincoln with the "original gorilla," a baboon, and a long-armed ape; the more scurrilous elements of the opposition party suggested that the President suffered from unmentionable diseases or that he had Negro blood in his veins.

If the President's failure with the Democrats was to be expected in a country with a vigorous two-party tradition, his inability to influence leaders of his own party was a more serious weakness. In Washington, reported Richard Henry Dana, author of *Two Years Before the Mast*, "the most striking thing is the absence of personal loyalty to the President. It does not exist. He has no admirers, no enthusiastic supporters, none to bet on his head." Republican critics openly announced that Lincoln was "unfit," a "political coward," a "dictator," "timid and ignorant," "pitiable," "too slow," a man

of "no education," "shattered, dazed, utterly foolish." "He is ignorant, self-willed, & is surrounded by men some of whom are almost
as ignorant as himself," historian George Bancroft declared. Republican editor Murat Halstead thought Lincoln "an awful, woeful
ass," and a correspondent of the Chicago *Tribune* said that
"Buchanan seems to have been a granite pillar compared to the
'Good natured man' without any spinal column. . . ." Republican
Senator James W. Grimes of Iowa felt that Lincoln's "entire administration has been a disgrace from the very beginning to every one
who had any thing to do with bringing it into power."

From the beginning the President and his own party leaders in
Congress were often at loggerheads. Radicals and Conservatives,
former Whigs and ex-Democrats, Easterners and Westerners, all
viewed Lincoln with suspicion. Such a situation is, of course, fairly
normal in American politics. As our major parties consist of conflicting interest groups bound together by political expediency
rather than by ideology, a President is bound constantly to disap-
point nine tenths of the voters who elected him. But in Lincoln's
case the situation was more serious because he seemed unable to
build up any personally loyal following. Nearly every important
Republican leader—Chase, Sumner, Greeley, Stevens, Wade,
Davis, Chandler, Browning, Grimes, Weed—doubted the advis-
ability of a second term for Lincoln. When a Pennsylvania editor
visited the Capitol in 1864 and asked to meet some Congressmen
who favored the President's renomination, old Thad Stevens
stumped over to Representative Isaac N. Arnold of Illinois,
announcing: "Here is a man who wants to find a Lincoln member
of Congress. You are the only one I know and I have come over to
introduce my friend to you."

A failure with the press and the politicians, Lincoln is said by
sentimentalists to have won the favor of the common people. This
stereotype, so comforting to those who like to believe in the democratic dogma, started with Lincoln himself. When Congressmen
and editors erupted in a frenzy of anti-Lincoln fury, the President
liked to reflect that the "politicians" could not "transfer the people,
the honest though misguided masses" to their course of opposition.

Lincoln felt that he understood the mind of the masses. Day after day he greeted the throngs of visitors, petitioners, and office-seekers who besieged him in the White House, and he claimed that these "public-opinion baths" helped him sense the popular will. In return for his sympathy, the President felt, he received popular support. His private secretary, John Hay, echoed Lincoln's belief: "The people know what they want and will have it"—namely, a re-election of the President in 1864.

In fact, though, the evidence for Lincoln's enormous popular appeal during the war is sketchy and unreliable. One could quote, for instance, Congressman Lewis D. Campbell's opinion of the 1864 election: "Nothing but the undying attachment of our people to the Union has saved us from terrible disaster. Mr. Lincoln's popularity had nothing to do with it. . . ." More convincing, however, than such impressionistic evidence are the actual election returns. Lincoln was a minority President in 1861. His party lost control of the crucial states of New York, Pennsylvania, Ohio, Indiana, and Illinois in the off-year elections of 1862. And in 1864—when all the Southern states were out of the Union and, of course, not voting— Northerners, given a chance to demonstrate their alleged enthusiastic support for the President, cast 45 percent of their ballots against Lincoln and for a Democratic platform that called both his administration and the war for the Union failures. A change of only 83,000 votes—2 percent of the total—could have meant Lincoln's defeat.

II

Although Lincoln failed to win the press, the politicians, and the people, he was nevertheless a successful politician. He kept himself and his party in power. He was the first President since Andrew Jackson to win re-election, and his administration began an unbroken twenty-four years of Republican control of the Presidency.

The secret of Lincoln's success is simple: he was an astute and dextrous operator of the political machine. Such a verdict at first seems almost preposterous, for one thinks of Lincoln's humility, so great as to cause his opponents to call him a "Uriah Heep"; of his frankness, which brought him the epithet "Honest Abe"; of his well-known aversion for what he termed the "details of how we get along." Lincoln carefully built up this public image of himself as a babe in the Washington wilderness. To a squabbling group of Pennsylvania party leaders he said ingenuously: "You know I never was a contriver; I don't know much about how things are done in politics. . . ."

Before breaking into tears of sympathy for this innocent among thieves, it is well to review Lincoln's prepresidential career. When elected President, he had been in active politics for twenty-six years; politics was his life. "He was an exceedingly ambitious man," his Springfield law partner wrote, "a man totally swallowed up in his ambitions. . . ." "Rouse Mr. Lincoln's peculiar nature in a point where he deeply felt—say in his ambitions—his general greed for office . . . then Mr. Lincoln preferred Abm Lincoln to anybody else." But during his long career in Illinois politics Lincoln had never been chosen to major office by the people of his state; state legislator and one-term member of Congress he was, but never Senator—though he twice tried unsuccessfully—and never Governor. Lack of appeal at the polls did not, however, prevent him from becoming the master wire-puller who operated the state political organization first of the Whig party and, after its decay, that of the Republicans. Behind that façade of humble directness and folksy humor, Lincoln was moving steadily toward his object; by 1860 he had maneuvered himself into a position where he controlled the party machinery, platform, and candidates of one of the pivotal states in the Union. A Chicago lawyer who had known Lincoln intimately for three decades summarized these prepresidential years: "One great public mistake . . . generally received and acquiesced in, is that he is considered by the people of this country as a frank, guileless, and unsophisticated man. There never was a greater mistake. . . . He handled and moved men remotely as we do pieces upon a chess-board."

Lincoln's Illinois record was merely finger exercises to the display of political virtuosity he was to exhibit in the White House. He brought to the Executive office an understanding of the value of secrecy. So close did Lincoln keep his ideas, it can be said that no one of his associates understood him. Herndon concluded that this man was "a profound mystery—an enigma—a sphinx—a riddle . . . incommunicative—silent—reticent—secretive—having profound policies—and well laid—deeply studied plans." Nobody had his complete confidence. His loyal Secretary of the Navy was kept as much in the dark about Lincoln's views as the veriest outsider. "Of the policy of the administration, if there be one," Welles complained, "I am not advised beyond what is published and known to all." Lincoln moved toward his objectives with muffled oars. Historians are still arguing whether Lincoln arranged for Andrew Johnson to be nominated as his vice-presidential running-mate in 1864. Impressive and suggestive evidence can be cited to show that the President picked the Tennessean—or that he favored someone else entirely.

Lincoln's renowned sense of humor was related to his passion for secrecy. Again and again self-important delegations would descend upon the White House, deliver themselves of ponderous utterances upon pressing issues of the war, and demand point-blank what the President proposed to do about their problems. Lincoln could say much in few words when he chose, but he could also say nothing at great length when it was expedient. His petitioners' request, he would say, reminded him of "a little story," which he would proceed to tell in great detail, accompanied by mimicry and gestures, by hearty slapping of the thigh, by uproarious laughter at the end—at which time he would usher out his callers, baffled and confused by the smoke screen of good humor, with their questions still unanswered.

Akin to Lincoln's gift for secrecy was his talent for passivity. When he arrived in Washington, he was faced by a crisis not of his own making. Fort Sumter, provocatively located in the harbor of Charleston, the very hotbed of secession, had to be reinforced or evacuated. Reinforcement would be interpreted, not merely by the Confederates but also by large peace-loving elements at the North, as an aggressive act of war; withdrawal would appear to other Northerners a cowardly retreat on the part of a spineless administration.

Lincoln considered both alternatives. Characteristically, he sought clear-cut written opinions from his Cabinet advisers on the course to follow—but left his own ideas unrecorded. Characteristically, the whole episode is muffled in a fog of confusion that has produced an interesting argument among later historians. But characteristically, too, Lincoln's final decision was neither to reinforce nor to withdraw; he would merely send food and supplies to the beleaguered Sumter garrison and sit back and wait. His passivity paid off. Confederate hotheads were unable to wait so long as the cool-blooded Northern President, and they fired the first shot at Sumter. To Lincoln's support all elements of Northern society now rallied. "At the darkest moment in the history of the republic," Ralph Waldo Emerson wrote, "when it looked as if the nation would be dismembered, pulverized into its original elements, the attack on Fort Sumter crystallized the North into a unit, and the hope of mankind was saved."

Repeatedly, throughout the war, Lincoln's passive policy worked politically. Because any action would offend somebody, he took as few actions as possible. Outright abolitionists demanded that he use his wartime powers to emancipate the Negroes. Border-state politicians insisted that he protect their peculiar institutions. Lincoln needed the support of both groups; therefore, he did nothing—or, rather, he proposed to colonize the Negroes in Central America, which was as near to nothing as he could come—and awaited events. After two years of hostilities, many even in the South came to see that slavery was doomed, and all the important segments of Northern opinion were brought to support emancipation as a wartime necessity. Only then did Lincoln issue the Emancipation Proclamation.

Along with secrecy and passivity, Lincoln brought to his office an extraordinarily frank pragmatism—some might call it opportunism. Often while in the White House he repeated an anecdote that seemed to have a special meaning for him—how the Irishman who had forsworn liquor told the bartender that he was not averse to having a spot added to his lemonade, "so long as it's unbeknownst to me." Again and again the President showed himself an imitator of his Irish hero. When the Pennsylvania miners broke out in open rebellion against the operation of the draft law in their section, worried Harrisburg officials inquired whether Lincoln would send troops to execute the law. Entrusting nothing to paper, Lincoln sent a confidential messenger to A. K. McClure, the aide of the Pennsylvania governor: "Say to McClure that I am very desirous to have the laws fully executed, but it might be well, in an extreme emergency, to be content with the appearance of executing the laws; I think McClure will understand." McClure did understand, and he made no more than a feeble effort to subdue the miners' revolt, but let the agitation die out of its own accord. Thus, the Lincoln administration won the credit both for preserving the peace and for enforcing the draft.

Lincoln enjoyed a similar pragmatic relationship with his unpleasant and irritable Secretary of War, Edwin M. Stanton. There was a sort of tacit division of labor between these two dissimilar men. Lincoln himself explained the system: ". . . I want to oblige everybody when I can; and Stanton and I have an understanding that if I send an order to him which cannot be consistently granted, he is to refuse it. This he sometimes does." The President then had the pleasant and politically rewarding opportunity of recommending promotions, endorsing pension applications, pardoning deserters, and saving sleeping sentinels, and Stanton, who was something of a sadist, took equal pleasure in refusing the promotions, ignoring the petitions, and executing the delinquent soldiers. While the Secretary received the blame for all the harsh and unpopular acts that war makes necessary, the President acquired a useful reputation for sympathy and generosity.

III

VALUABLE as were these negative traits of secrecy, passivity, and pragmatism, Lincoln understood that it was not policies or principles which would cause Congressmen to support his direction of the war. To mobilize votes in Congress, the Head of State must be a practicing Party Leader. Lincoln was a political realist, and he worked with the tools he had at hand. He understood that in a democratic, federal government like ours, patronage is the one sure way of binding local political bosses to the person and principles of the President, and for this reason he used and approved the spoils system.

Lincoln's entire administration was characterized by astute handling of the patronage. Even in picking his Cabinet, he took leaders from all factions of his own party, giving all groups hope but no group dominance. The result was that Cabinet members were so suspicious of one another that they hardly had time to be jealous of the President. It was not efficient administration. Secretary of State Seward tried to bypass Secretary of the Navy Gideon Welles and give orders directly to naval commanders, and for a time he virtually took over the running of Simon Cameron's War Department. Postmaster General Montgomery Blair distrusted Seward and disliked Stanton, Cameron's successor. Treasury Secretary Chase was suspicious of all of his colleagues. Of all these men, outstanding political leaders in 1860, not one ever became President; in Lincoln's Cabinet they ate one another up.

Even without such competition, a Cabinet officer found his political activity necessarily curbed. The fading of Salmon P. Chase's presidential hopes provides an illuminating insight into Lincoln's use of the appointing power. Self-confident, upright, and able, Chase thought that he had deserved the Republican nomination in 1860, and from the first the Secretary of the Treasury looked upon Lincoln as a well-meaning incompetent. He never saw reason to alter his view. Chase was not a modest man; he was sure of his ability and his integrity, sure that he would make an admirable President. As a Senator said: "Chase is a good man, but his theology is unsound. He thinks there is a fourth person in the Trinity" — namely, himself.

The day he became Secretary of the Treasury, Chase began scheming for the 1864 nomination, but he found himself hampered by his ambiguous position in the Cabinet. If his financial planning went wrong, he received the blame; but whenever he achieved a success, in the issue of greenbacks or the sale of bonds, the credit went to the Lincoln administration, not to Chase alone. He converted his numerous Treasury agents into a tightly organized and highly active Chase-for-President league, but as long as he remained in the Cabinet, he could not openly announce his presidential aspirations. To relieve himself from embarrassment, to go into outright opposition to Lincoln, Chase needed to get out of the Cabinet, but an unprovoked resignation would be political suicide, a cowardly evasion of his duties. All through 1863 and 1864, then, Chase wriggled and squirmed. Time after time he cooked up little quarrels over patronage, squabbles over alleged slights, and the like, so that he would have an excuse for resigning. Every time Lincoln blandly yielded the point in dispute and refused to accept Chase's withdrawal. But in June 1864, just after the Republican national convention at Baltimore had renominated Lincoln, Chase once again tried his obstructionist tactics that had worked so well in the past, and he threatened to resign from the Cabinet. This time, to his vast chagrin, it was different, and Lincoln accepted his withdrawal. Now that the race was over, Chase was free to run.

If patronage could close a Cabinet member's mouth, it could open the lips of an editor. James Gordon Bennett, the sinful and unscrupulous editor of the New York *Herald*, was one of the most powerful newspapermen of his day. Spiced with sex and scandal, the *Herald* had the largest circulation of any American newspaper, and it was a potent agency in shaping public opinion. Bennett had opposed Lincoln in 1860, and throughout the war he kept up a criticism that was all the more painful to Lincoln because it was well informed and witty. In 1864 Bennett hoped that Grant would run for President, and he also flirted capriciously with the Democratic nominee, General McClellan. For Lincoln he had no use.

President Lincoln [read a typical *Herald* editorial] is a joke incarnated. His election was a very sorry joke. The idea that such a man as he should be President of such a country as this is a very ridiculous joke.... His inaugural address was a joke, since it was full of promises which he has never performed. His Cabinet is and always has been a standing joke. All his State papers are jokes. . . . His title of "Honest" is a satirical joke. . . . His intrigues to secure a renomination and the hopes he appears to entertain of a re-election are, however, the most laughable jokes of all.

The vote in New York was going to be close, and Lincoln needed the *Herald*'s support. Emissaries went up from Washington to interview the canny Scottish editor and ascertain his price. Bennett's terms were high. "The fact is B. wants attention," Lincoln's agent reported. "He wants recognition—& I think it will pay." A newspaperman before he was anything else, Bennett promised to give the administration's views "a thorough exposition in the columns of the Herald," provided Lincoln and his advisers "would occasionally confidentially make known to him [their] plans." Then, too, the editor, who was barred from polite New York society because of his flagrant immorality and was generally considered "too pitchy to touch," had a hankering for social respectability. When Lincoln's agents approached him, the editor "asked plumply, 'Will I be a welcome visitor at the White House if I support Mr. Lincoln?'" The answer was unequivocally affirmative, and, as proof of his good faith, the President promised to the totally unqualified Bennett an appointment as minister to France. Bennett did not want to go abroad, for he was too busy with his paper, but he did want the social recognition that such an offer implied; he wanted to be able to refuse. The bargain was complete, and the *Herald* abandoned its criticism of the President.

As a practical politician, Lincoln understood that election victories required more than the support of Cabinet officers or newspaper editors. Like a famous New York politician, he knew that "Parties are not built up by deportment, or by ladies' magazines, or gush." In the United States, party machinery is more important than public opinion, and patronage more influential than principles. In recent years American liberal historians, scorning the sordid realities of political life, have pictured Lincoln as somehow above the vulgar party apparatus that elected him, unconcerned with the greasy machinery of party caucuses, conventions, nominations, and patronage. This idea is the political equivalent of the doctrine of the immaculate conception. Lincoln himself would have been astonished at it. Politics was his life, and he was a regular party man. Long before he became President, Lincoln said that "the man who is of neither party is not, and cannot be, of any consequence" in American life. As Chief Executive, he was a party President, and he proudly claimed that his had "distributed to it's party friends as nearly all the civil patronage as any administration ever did."

Lincoln believed in party regularity. In 1864 there was much discontent in New York with Representative Roscoe Conkling, a Radical Republican who sought re-election, and more moderate party members threatened to bolt the ticket. Conkling was no personal friend of Lincoln's. Boasting the "finest torso" in American political life, he used to descend upon the harried inmate of the White House and, with his wilting contempt, "his haughty disdain, his grandiloquent swell, his majestic, supereminent, turkey-gobbler strut," proceed to lecture the President on how to conduct the war. But Conkling in 1864 was the nominee of the New York Republican party, and the President wrote a public letter to aid him:

> . . . I am for the regular nominee in all cases; . . . and no one could be more satisfactory to me as the nominee in that District, than Mr. Conkling. I do not mean to say that there [are] not others as good as he is in the District; but I think I know him to be at least good enough.

Lincoln made the politicos pay for his support. They could vote against administration bills and they could grumble in Capitol cloakrooms about presidential "imbecility," but he expected them to support his renomination. Those who refused were cut off from patronage and promotion. When Senator Samuel C. Pomeroy of Kansas tried to organize the Chase boom in 1864, every patronage plum in his state was snatched from his greedy hands. After a few months of dignified hostility, Pomeroy sidled up to the White

House and begged forgiveness. But Lincoln, who could be so forgiving to sleeping sentinels and deserting soldiers, had no mercy for defecting politicians, and Pomeroy went hungry.

Using the sure goad of patronage, Lincoln's agents early in 1864 began lining up delegates to the Republican national convention. Before the other presidential hopefuls knew that the round-up had begun, Lincoln had corralled enough votes to insure his renomination. The work of the Lincoln men in a state like New Hampshire is instructive. Dignified Salmon P. Chase was making eyes toward this state where he had been born, but while he was still flirting at a gentlemanly distance, New Hampshire eloped with Lincoln. Shrewd Lincoln agents, dispensing patronage to the faithful and threats of punishment to the disobedient, moved in on the state convention at Concord in January 1864 and rushed through a resolution calling for Lincoln's renomination. They permitted New Hampshire Republicans to mention their native son, Chase, in the state platform—but only in order to urge that he clean up the corruption in his Treasury Department.

Everywhere it was the same—Connecticut, Pennsylvania, New York, and even Chase's own Ohio. From state after state Chase's friends protested: "I have never seen such an exhibition of office holders in any convention before." But, packed or not, these conventions chose the delegates to the national assembly at Baltimore. By March Lincoln's renomination was assured, and, with poor grace, Chase was compelled to withdraw from a hopeless contest.

Patronage had helped defeat Lincoln's enemies within the Republican party, and patronage would help defeat the Democratic nominee, George B. McClellan. No one knows how much money the Republicans spent in the 1864 campaign—indeed, no one knows how much either major party has spent in any campaign—but it is certain that a large part of the sum came from assessments levied upon Federal officeholders. A man who received a job from Lincoln might expect to contribute regularly 10 percent of his income to the Republican campaign chest; some gave much more. Henry J. Raymond, chairman of the Republican National Committee, planned systematically to levy upon war contractors, customs officers, and navy-yard employees. When the upright Secretary of the Navy protested this proposal "to take the organization of the navy yard into their keeping, to name the Commandant, to remove the Naval Constructor, to change the regulations, and make the yard a party machine for the benefit of party, and to employ men to elect candidates instead of building ships," Raymond summoned him into the President's office in the White House and gave the Secretary a little lecture on the political facts of life, with Lincoln silently approving each word.

In the long run, though, it took not merely delegates and money but votes to carry the election. During the summer of 1864 the war was going badly. "I am a beaten man," Lincoln said in August, "unless we can have some great victory." As late as October he calculated that he would carry the electoral college by only six votes—three of them from the barren desert of Nevada, which Lincoln leaders in Congress had providently admitted to the Union precisely for such an emergency.

Although propriety prevented him from campaigning, the President personally concerned himself with the turnout of Republican voters in key states like Indiana, Ohio, Pennsylvania, and New York. Seeing that the Northwestern states were going to show a closely balanced vote, Lincoln wrote in September to General Sherman, whose army was in a tight spot in Georgia: "Any thing you can safely do to let [your] soldiers, or any part of them, go home to vote at the State election, will be greatly in point." Although he added, "This is, in no sense, an order," Lincoln was clearly giving a directive, and it was one that Sherman promptly obeyed. The Republicans carried the Northwest by narrow majorities.

In the East, too, the soldier vote was crucial. Pennsylvania Republicans, fearing defeat, persuaded the President to furlough thousands of soldiers just in time to return home and vote. When the ballots were counted, Lincoln had carried the state by only twenty thousand and would have lost it entirely but for the army. In New York the soldier influence on the election was somewhat different. There, allegedly to prevent rioting, daredevil Republican General Benjamin F. Butler was put in charge of Federal troops and, over the protests of New York officials, he stationed plain-clothesmen at the polling places and had four regiments of troops waiting on ferryboats, ready to "land and march double quick across the island"—just in case there were Democratic distur-bances. Some years later, reviewing his career, Butler denied that he had earned his military laurels in the Louisiana campaign. ". . . I do not claim," he said modestly, "to be the hero of New Orleans. Farragut has that high honor; but I do claim to be the hero of New York city in the election of 1864, when they had an honest election, the only one before or since." A Democrat might question the "honesty" of the proceedings, but, under the protection of Federal bayonets, New York went Republican by seven thousand votes.

November 8 was a "rainy, steamy and dark" night in Washing-ton, but politicians gathered in the War Department to await the telegraphic election returns. Most of the visitors were tense, but Abraham Lincoln was relaxed, "most agreeable and genial all the evening." At a little midnight supper he "went awkwardly and hos-pitably to work shoveling out the fried oysters" to others, and more than once he was reminded of a little story. A mishap to one of the guests brought to mind an anecdote about wrestling that began: "For such an awkward fellow, I am pretty sure-footed. It used to take a pretty dextrous man to throw me." His political management of the Civil War demonstrated that Abraham Lincoln was still sure-footed. By dominating his party, securing a renomination, and win-ning re-election, a superb politician had gained the opportunity of becoming a superb statesman.

BIBLIOGRAPHICAL ESSAY

ONE

Getting Right With Lincoln

THIS ESSAY ORIGINALLY APPEARED in *Harper's Magazine*, CII (April 1951), 74–80, and I am grateful to the editors of that publication for permission to reprint it here.

The best guide to the tedious literature of Lincoln eulogy is Jay Monaghan's elaborate *Lincoln Bibliography, 1839–1939* (1945), which lists 3,958 books and pamphlets, including hundreds of sermons and campaign speeches in which the Great Emancipator is invoked. This essay is based chiefly upon a sampling of these titles and upon a careful reading of the New York *Times* files from 1887 to 1948. For a brilliant history of the Lincoln legend after that date see Merrill D. Peterson, *Lincoln in American Memory* (1994).

For the partisan manipulation of the Lincoln symbol in the months immediately following his assassination, I have relied heavily upon a master's thesis prepared at Columbia University under my direction by Lewis Clish. Sumner's appeal to Lincoln's memory is found in the Senator's *Works*, IX (1875), 367–428; reactions appear in numerous letters to Sumner in the Charles Sumner MSS., Harvard College Library. On political squabbling during the Reconstruction, Howard K. Beale, *The Critical Year* (1930), and George Fort Milton, *The Age of Hate* (1930), are helpful. Boutwell's effusion on Lincoln is found in his *Reminiscences of Sixty Years in Public Affairs* (1902); Cleveland's statement is in Allan Nevins, ed., *Letters of Grover Cleveland* (1933); and Colonel McCormick's animadversions are in *An Address . . . February 12, 1936*. For Franklin D. Roosevelt's frequent appeal to Lincolnian precedent see S. I. Rosenman, ed., *Public Papers and Addresses of Franklin D. Roosevelt* (1938–50).

Lloyd Lewis's *Myths after Lincoln* (1929) is valuable on the "Black Easter" of Lincoln's death. Roy P. Basler, *The Lincoln Legend* (1935), is also useful, though it emphasizes the literary rather than the political use of the myths. In *Lincoln's Herndon* (1948) I tried to establish a connection between biographers' political affiliations and their interpretations of Lincoln.

TWO

The Folklore Lincoln

This essay originally appeared in the *Journal of the Illinois State Historical Society*, XL (1947), 377–86. I am indebted to the editors of that publication for permission to republish it. For a recent searching analysis that addresses some of the same issues see David W. Blight, *Race and Reunion: The Civil War in American Memory* (2000).

On the Lincoln myth many of the sources listed for the previous essay remain pertinent. For African-American versions of the myth see B. A. Botkin, ed., *Lay My Burden Down* (1945), and John E. Washington, *They Knew Lincoln* (1942). White Southerners' views are examined in Avery Craven, "Southern Attitudes toward Abraham Lincoln," *Papers in Illinois History, 1942*, pp. 1–18.

Benjamin P. Thomas's *Portrait for Posterity* (1947) is an excellent guide to Lincoln biography; it is accurate, amusing, and informative. For the picture of Lincoln as demigod, nothing will replace a reading of Josiah G. Holland's *The Life of Abraham Lincoln* (1866). Far more engrossing is William H. Herndon and Jesse W. Weik, *Herndon's Lincoln: The True Story of a Great Life* (1889). I have studied the sources of Herndon's book and have analyzed its reliability in my *Lincoln's Herndon* (1948).

Most of my quotations from spurious or distorted "recollections" about Lincoln come from the invaluable files of the Lincoln Museum in Fort Wayne, Indiana.

On the general subject of folklore and its usefulness for historians I have profited by consultations with Professor Florian Znaniecki of the University of Illinois, with Dr. Robert Price of Otterbein College, authority on Johnny Appleseed, and with Dr. Milo M. Quaife of the Detroit Public Library. My thinking has also been shaped by Lord Raglan, *The Hero: A Study in Tradition, Myth, and Drama* (1936); Dixon Wecter, *The Hero in America* (1941); W. A. Dunning, "Truth in History," *American Historical Review*, XIX (1914), 217–29; and Ralph H. Gabriel, *The Course of American Democratic Thought* (1943).

THREE

Toward a Reconsideration of Abolitionists

The best general discussion of the age of reform is Alice Felt Tyler's entertaining *Freedom's Ferment* (1944). Louis Filler, *The Crusade Against Slavery, 1830–1860* (1960), gives an excellent overview. Other valuable studies include Gilbert H. Barnes, *The Antislavery Impulse, 1830–1844* (1933), Dwight L. Dumond, *Antislavery Origins of the Civil War in the United States* (1939), Aileen S. Kraditor, *Means and Ends in American Abolitionism* (1969), James Brewer Stewart, *Holy Warriors: The Abolitionists and American Slavery* (1976), Peter Walker, *Moral Choices: Memory and Desire in Nineteenth-Century American Abolition* (1978), and Ronald G. Walters, *The Antislavery Appeal* (1976). A number of these studies do not agree with the thesis of my essay.

Older biographies of abolitionists, like *William Lloyd Garrison, 1805–1870: The Story of His Life Told by His Children* (1885–89), heavily overemphasized the Garrisonian fringe. Three impressive modern biographies are Henry Mayer, *All On Fire: William Lloyd Garrison and the Abolition of Slavery* (1998), Walter M. Merrill, *Against Wind and Tide: A Biography of William Lloyd Garrison* (1963), and John L. Thomas, *The Liberator, William Lloyd Garrison*

(1963). Other excellent studies of abolitionist leaders include Irving H. Bartlett, *Wendell Phillips: Brahmin Radical* (1961), Betty Fladeland, *James Gillespie Birney: Slaveholder to Abolitionist* (1955), Benjamin P. Thomas, *Theodore Weld: Crusader for Freedom* (1950), and Bertram Wyatt-Brown, *Lewis Tappan and the Evangelical War Against Slavery* (1969).

In preparing this essay I found particularly useful William Charvat's "American Romanticism and the Depression of 1837," *Science and Society*, II (1937), 67–82. On the relation of religion to reform, the best study is Whitney Cross's *The Burned-Over District* (1950). Frank Tracy Carlton's *Economic Influences upon Educational Progress in the United States, 1820–1850* (1908) is suggestive.

FOUR

An Excess of Democracy

This essay was my inaugural lecture as Harmsworth Professor of American History at the University of Oxford, and it is reprinted with the kind permission of the Oxford University Press.

The best guides to the historiography on the causes of the Civil War are Howard K. Beale, "What Historians Have Said About the Causes of the Civil War," in *Theory and Practice in Historical Study* (Social Science Research Council *Bulletin*, no. 54 [1946]), 55–102, and Thomas J. Pressly, *Americans Interpret Their Civil War* (1954).

Alexis de Tocqueville's *Democracy in America*, ed. by Phillips Bradley (1945), remains basic for any understanding of American thought and life in the nineteenth century. The best studies of the relationship between character and culture include Stanley Elkins, *Slavery: A Problem in American Institutional and Intellectual Life* (1959), Robert Kelley, *The Cultural Pattern in American Politics: The First Century* (1979), Edward Pessen, *Riches, Class and Power: American Life before the Civil War* (1989), David M. Potter, *People of Plenty: Economic Abundance and the American Character* (1954), and Robert W. Wiebe, *The Opening of American Society* (1984). For a sampling of travelers' judgments on American society see Warren S. Tryon, ed., *A Mirror for Americans* (3 vols., 1952); for the views of European observers consult Oscar Handlin, *This Was America* (1949).

FIVE

Education Defective

The literature about Lincoln's education is slim. His own statements on his schooling may be found in Roy P. Basler and others, eds., The *Collected Works of Abraham Lincoln* (9 vols., 1953–55). See especially his autobiographical statements, *ibid.*, II, 459, III, 511–12, and IV, 60–67.

For recollections by Mrs. Thomas Lincoln, Dennis Hanks, John Hanks, and others of Lincoln's schooling and reading, see Douglas L. Wilson and Rodney O. Davis, eds., *Herndon's Informants: Letters, Interviews, and Statements about Abraham Lincoln* (1998). Albert J. Beveridge, *Abraham Lincoln, 1809–1858* (1928), I, 70–77, gives a full account of Lincoln's reading, but it should be supplemented by Louis A. Warren, *Lincoln's Youth: Indiana Years, Seven to Twenty-One, 1816–1830* (1959). Douglas L. Wilson, "What Jefferson and Lincoln Read," *Atlantic Monthly*, CCLXVII (January 1991), 151–62, is thoughtful. There is much useful information in M. L. Houser, *Lincoln's Education and Other Essays* (1957).

I have relied heavily on an excellent article by Maurice Dorfman, "Lincoln's Arithmetic Education: Influence on His Life," *Lincoln Herald*, LVIII (Summer 1966), 61–80. Lloyd A. Dunlap, "Lincoln's Sum Book,'" *Lincoln Herald*, LXI (Spring 1959), 6–10, is also useful.

Lawrence A. Cremin, American Education: The National Experience, 1783–1876 (1980), is a masterful overview. Bernard Bailyn, *Education in the Forming of American Society* (1960), is important and provocative.

SIX

Herndon and Mary Lincoln

This essay originally appeared, in a slightly different form, in *Books at Brown*, XII (April 1950), and I am indebted to the librarian of Brown University for permission to reprint it here.

My *Lincoln's Herndon* (1948) remains the only biography of Lincoln's law partner and biographer. The materials he collected for a biography of Lincoln have been published in Douglas L. Wilson and Rodney O. Davis, eds., *Herndon's Informants: Letters, Interviews, and Statements about Abraham Lincoln* (1998). A selection of Herndon's own ruminations about Lincoln and his wife appears in Emanuel Hertz, ed., *The Hidden Lincoln* (1938). Herndon put forth his exaggerated account of the Ann Rutledge story in *Abraham Lincoln. Miss Ann Rutledge. New Salem. Pioneering, and THE Poem* (1866). A somewhat more restrained account appeared in William H. Herndon and Jesse W. Weik, *Herndon's Lincoln: The True Story of a Great Life* (1889). Though widely accepted by earlier biographers, the Ann Rutledge story came under devastating criticism, most notably in J. G. Randall, *Lincoln the President: Springfield to Gettysburg* (1945), II, 321–42. *Lincoln's Herndon* shared that skepticism. Recently, however, I have come to adopt a more tolerant view of this episode, which I have presented in my *Lincoln* (1995). An elaborate note (pp. 608–9) explains the reasons for the change and lists some of the important recent literature on the subject.

To understand Mrs. Lincoln one must begin with *Mary Todd Lincoln: Her Life and Letters*, ed. by Justin G. Turner and Linda Levitt Turner (1972). For the letters she and her husband exchanged, see my *Lincoln at Home: Two Glimpses of Lincoln's Domestic Life* (2000). The best biography is Jean Harvey Baker, *Mary Todd Lincoln* (1987). Ruth P. Randall, *Mary Lincoln: Biography of a Marriage* (1953), is more detailed but less critical. W. A. Evans, *Mrs. Abraham Lincoln* (1932), and Katherine Helm, *True Story of Mary, Wife of Lincoln* (1928), contain useful insights.

SEVEN
Refighting the Civil War

Some of the best writing on the military history of the Civil War is by British experts, who have given greater attention to military theory. The following important articles appeared in *The Army Quarterly:* E. W. Sheppard, "Policy and Command in the American Civil War, 1864–1865," XXXVII (1939), 294–303; Liddell Hart, "The Psychology of a Commander. General R. E. Lee . . . ," XXX (1935), 50–58, 206–16; J. C. F. Fuller, "A Study of Mobility in the American Civil War," XXIX (1935), 261–71; and Fuller, "The Place of the American Civil War in the Evolution of War," XXVI (1933), 316–25.

Other important studies by British authorities are: Michael C. C. Adams, *Our Masters the Rebels* (1978); Colin R. Ballard, *The Military Genius of Abraham Lincoln* (1926); A. H. Burne, *Lee, Grant and Sherman* (1938); Cyril Falls, *A Hundred Years of War* (1953); J. C. F. Fuller, *The Generalship of Grant* (1929) and *Grant and Lee* (1933); G. R. F. Henderson, *Stonewall Jackson and the American Civil War* (1936); and Frederick Maurice, *Robert E. Lee the Soldier* (1925) and *Statesmen and Soldiers of the Civil War* (1926).

Of the many earlier American interpretations of Civil War strategy I have found the following most helpful: Douglas S. Freeman, *R. E. Lee* (1934–35); Kenneth P. William, *Lincoln Finds a General* (1949–59); and T. Harry Williams, *Lincoln and His Generals* (1952). More recent writers on the Civil War, in books published since the original appearance of this essay, have paid more attention to military theory. Some of the best are: Richard E. Beringer, et al., *Why the South Lost the Civil War* (1986); Gabor S. Boritt, ed., *Why the Confederacy Lost* (1992); Edward Hagerman, *The American Civil War and the Origins of Modern Warfare* (1988); Herman Hattaway and Archer Jones, *How the North Won* (1991); and Grady McWhiney and Perry D. Jamieson, *Attack and Die: Civil War Military Tactics and the Southern Heritage* (1982).

EIGHT

The Radicals and Lincoln

The position challenged in this essay was one held for more than a generation by most Civil War historians. It was most clearly and emphatically expressed in T. Harry Williams, *Lincoln and the Radicals* (1941), but was a fundamental thesis in such works as J. G. Randall and R. N. Current, *Lincoln the President* (1945–55), W. B. Hesseltine, *Lincoln and the War Governors* (1948), and Benjamin P. Thomas, *Abraham Lincoln* (1952).

For fuller, elaborately documented statements of my thesis see "Devils Facing Zionwards," in Grady McWhiney, ed., *Grant, Lee, Lincoln and the Radicals* (1964), 72–91; *Charles Sumner and the Rights of Man* (1970); and *Lincoln* (1995). This interpretation has now been widely accepted. See, for example, Hans L. Trefousse's admirable *The Radical Republicans: Lincoln's Vanguard for Racial Justice* (1969). In two important books Allan G. Bogue has presented an analysis of the legislative branch: *The Congressman's Civil War* (1989) and *The Earnest Men: Republicans of the Civil War Senate* (1981). Michael Les Benedict, *A Compromise of Principle* (1974), is an important study of Republican factionalism.

On the Cabinet "round robin," allegedly designed to curb Lincoln, see my edition of Salmon P. Chase's diaries, *Inside Lincoln's Cabinet* (1954). My account of the senatorial caucus of December 1862 is based chiefly upon Francis Fessenden, *Life and Public Services of William Pitt Fessenden* (1907). For Sumner's public statements on Lincoln see his "Promises of the Declaration of Independence, and Abraham Lincoln," in the Senator's *Works*, IX (1875), 367–428, and Edward L. Pierce, *Memoir and Letters of Charles Sumner* (1878–93). Most of my quotations from Sumner, however, come from manuscript sources. Lincoln's notes to Sumner are found in Basler, *The Collected Works of Abraham Lincoln* (1953–55). Carl Schurz's view of Sumner's relations to Lincoln appears in his *Reminiscences* (1907–8) and in his *Charles Sumner: An Essay* (Arthur R. Hogue, ed., 1951). On Sumner and Mrs. Lincoln, see Ruth P. Randall's *Mary Lincoln: Biography of a Marriage* (1953). Count Adam Gurowski's *Diary* (1862–66) has some animadversions upon the Lincoln-Sumner relationship, as does that of John Hay. For the scene at the second Inaugural Ball, consult the Count de Chambrun's *Impressions of Lincoln and the Civil War* (1952).

NINE

Abraham Lincoln and the American Pragmatic Tradition

The principal source for Lincoln's political philosophy is, of course, Lincoln's own writings, and this essay evolved as I was giving a word-by-word reading to *The Collected Works of Abraham Lincoln,* edited by Roy P. Basler and others (1953–55), in order to prepare a detailed, technical appraisal that appeared in the *American Historical Review,* LIX (1953), 142–49. In some ways my ideas run parallel to those found in two other review-articles on *The Collected Works*—T. Harry Williams's "Abraham Lincoln: Principle and Pragmatism in Politics," *Mississippi Valley Historical Review,* XL (1953), 89–106, and Edmund Wilson, "Abraham Lincoln: The Union as Religious Mysticism," in *Eight Essays* (1954).

Most writers on Lincoln's political ideas tell more about themselves than they do about the President. Outstanding exceptions are Vernon L. Parrington, "Lincoln: Free-Soil Liberal," in *Main Currents in American Thought* (1927), II, 152–60; Stanley Pargellis, "Lincoln's Political Philosophy," *Abraham Lincoln Quarterly,* III (1945), 275–90; and J. G. Randall, *Lincoln the Liberal Statesman* (1947), 175–206—essays with which I strongly disagree, but from which I have learned a great deal. Richard Hofstadter's "Abraham Lincoln and the Self-Made Myth," in his *The American Political Tradition* (1948), is brilliant and provocative. Allan Nevins's *The Statesmanship of the Civil War* (1953) is a thoughtful, eloquent appraisal of Lincoln.

TEN
A Whig in the White House

This essay first appeared in Norman A. Graebner, ed., *The Endur- ing Lincoln* (1959), and it is reprinted through the kind permission of the University of Illinois Press.

For conflicting views of Lincoln as wartime President see J. G. Randall, *Constitutional Problems under Lincoln* (1951), Wilfred E. Binkley, *President and Congress* (1947), Edward S. Corwin, *The President: Office and Powers* (1957), and Clinton Rossiter, *The American Presidency* (1956). Three excellent recent studies are: Herman Belz, *Lincoln and the Constitution: The Dictatorship Question Reconsidered* (1984); James M. McPherson, *Abraham Lincoln and the Second American Revolution* (1991); and Sidney M. Milkis and Michael Nelson, *The American Presidency: Origins and Development, 1776–1993* (1994).

A previous generation of historians was not much interested in the Whig party and its ideology. Even Leonard D. White in his authoritative administrative history, *The Jacksonians* (1954), gave the Whigs only minimal space. Recently, however, Daniel Walker Howe, *The Political Culture of the American Whigs* (1979), and Michael F. Holt, *The Rise and Fall of the American Whig Party* (1999), have refocused attention on the party. Gabor S. Boritt's *Lin- coln and the Economics of the American Dream* (1978) is the author- itative analysis of how Whig ideas, especially on economic issues, shaped Lincoln's thinking.

Recent important re-examinations of Lincoln's use of the war powers include: Herman Belz, *Emancipation and Equal Rights: Politics and Constitutionalism in the Civil War Era* (1978); Belz, *Reconstructing the Union: Theory and Policy during the Civil War* (1969); Harold M. Hyman, *A More Perfect Union: The Impact of the Civil War and Reconstruction* (1973); Hyman and William M. Wiecek, *Equal Justice under Law: Constitutional Development, 1835–1875* (1982); Phillip S. Paludan, *"A People's Contest": The Union and the Civil War* (1988); and, especially, Paludan, *A Con-*

venant with Death: The Constitution, Law, and Equality in the Civil War Era (1975).

ELEVEN
Reverence for the Laws

J. G. Randall's essay "The Rule of 'Law under Lincoln" first appeared in *Historical Outlook*, XVII (1926), 272–76. It was republished, with extensive revisions, in Randall, *Lincoln the Liberal Statesman* (1947), 118–34.

On Lincoln as a lawyer, see my *Lincoln* (1995), especially Chapter VI. Lincoln's 1838 lyceum lecture, "The Perpetuation of Our Political Institutions," can be found in Roy P. Basler and others, eds., *The Collected Works of Abraham Lincoln* (1953–55), I, 108–15.

For a hostile account of Lincoln's respect for law during the Civil War see Dean Sprague, *Freedom under Lincoln* (1965). Mark E. Neely, *The Fate of Liberty: Abraham Lincoln and Civil Liberties* (1991), is a thorough, balanced account. Robert S. Harper, *Lincoln and the Press* (1951), covers the rare cases when newspapers were censored or suspended.

On dissent and disloyalty in the North during wartime the standard accounts for many years were Wood Gray, *The Hidden Civil War: The Story of the Copperheads* (1942), and George F. Milton, *Abraham Lincoln and the Fifth Column* (1942). But Frank L. Klement in *The Copperheads in the Middle West* (1960) and *Dark Lanterns: Secret Political Societies, Conspiracies, and Treason Trials in the Civil War* (1984), and Kenneth M. Stampp in *Indiana Politics During the Civil War* (1949) present powerful evidence that few of the so-called Copperheads were disloyal. For the Vallandigham affair see Frank L. Klement, *The Limits of Dissent: Clement L. Vallandigham and the Civil War* (1970).

On Lincoln's "instrumental" views of the Constitution, which have been endorsed by many leading scholars, see the works by Belz, Hyman, Paludan, and Wiecek, cited above in the references for "A Whig in the White House."

TWELVE

A. Lincoln, Politician

Lincoln's political tactics are, of course, discussed in all his biographies, but none is so full and so perceptive as J. G. Randall and Richard N. Current, *Lincoln the President* (1945–55). I have also found William B. Hesseltine's *Lincoln and the War Governors* (1948) especially useful. The authoritative account of the 1864 election is David E. Long, *The Jewel of Liberty: Abraham Lincoln's Reelection and the End of Slavery* (1994), which I wish had been available to me when I was writing this essay.

For Lincoln's own writings on politics the best source is Roy P. Basler's edition of *The Collected Works of Abraham Lincoln* (1953–55), but some of his most important statements, significantly enough, were never put in writing. Thurlow Weed's *Life . . . , Including his Autobiography and a Memoir* (Harriet A. Weed, ed., 1883–84) contains Lincoln's proposition to Governor Seymour. Very revealing disclosures are made in Alexander K. McClure's *Abraham Lincoln and Men of War-Times* (1892) and *Lincoln as a Politician* (1916). For Herndon's view of Lincoln's political sagacity, see *Herndon's Lincoln* (1889) and Emanuel Hertz, *The Hidden Lincoln* (1938).

Some idea of Lincoln's unpopularity among his contemporaries may be gained from Robert S. Harper's *Lincoln and the Press* (1951) and from J. G. Randall's "The Unpopular Mr. Lincoln," in his *Lincoln the Liberal Statesman* (1947). On emancipation Randall's *Lincoln and the South* (1946) is suggestive. Problems of appointments are thoroughly treated in Harry J. Carman and Reinhard H. Luthin, *Lincoln and the Patronage* (1943). Although I cannot agree with his conclusion that Lincoln had a vast following among the common people, I am much indebted to William F. Zornow's *Lincoln and the Party Divided* (1954), a study of the 1864 election. An admirable master's thesis prepared under my direction, David Q. Voigt's "'Too Pitchy to Touch' — President Lincoln and Editor Bennett," *Abraham Lincoln Quarterly*, VI (1950), 139–61, discusses Lincoln's relations with the New York *Herald*.

Contemporary diaries have much to say about Lincoln's political operations. Howard K. Beale and Alan W. Brownsword, eds., *Diary of Gideon Welles* (1960) is the record of a Lincoln supporter who was sometimes shocked by the flagrant use of patronage. My edition of Salmon P. Chase's diaries, *Inside Lincoln's Cabinet* (1954), gives the reactions of an avowed competitor for the Republican nomination in 1864. Tyler Dennett's *Lincoln and the Civil War in the Letters and Diaries of John Hay* (1939) is my source for Lincoln's remarks on election night.

The full story of undercover Civil War political maneuvering can be traced only by examining the manuscript letters of participants. I have found particularly revealing the Robert Todd Lincoln Collection, Library of Congress; Charles Sumner MSS., Harvard College Library; Salmon P. Chase MSS., Historical Society of Pennsylvania and Library of Congress; Theodore Tilton MSS., New York Historical Society; and Francis Lieber MSS., Henry E. Huntington Library.

INDEX

Abolitionism, differentiated from
other antislavery movements,
32; suggested reasons for rise, 33;
influenced by revivalism, 34–5;
influenced by British precedent, 35; leadership analyzed,
35–6; sociological explanation
of origin, 36ff.
Abolitionists, criticize Lincoln, 31–2;
list of leaders compiled, 36;
average age, 36; identified with
New England, 36; ancestry,
36–7; economic status, 37;
education, 37–8; sex, 38; religious beliefs, 38; rural origin,
38; views on urban problems,
38–9; attitudes toward manufacturing, 39; political affiliations,
40; composite portrait, 39–40;
motivation, 42–3; reasons for
hostility to Lincoln, 43; rebuked
by Lincoln, 134
Adams, Charles Francis, favors
antislavery crusade, 109–10

Adams, Henry, 45
Adams, John, 150
Adams, John Quincy, on war powers
of President, 145–6
Aesop's *Fables*, 68
Amory, Cleveland, 51
Andrews, C. C., quoted, 52
Antietam, Battle of, 35, 97
Argyll, Duke and Duchess of, friends
of Sumner, 118
Arkansas, reconstruction in, 136
Arnold, Isaac N., writes Lincoln
biography, 26; only Lincoln
supporter in Congress, 168
Ashley, James M., welcomes death of
Lincoln, 4
Atlanta, campaign for, 101
Averell, William W., 101

Bagehot, Walter, quoted, 57–8
Bailyn, Bernard, 71
Baldwin, Joseph G., quoted, 52–4
Ballard, Colin, 89